Lawn Tennis
THE GREAT ONES

Lawn Tennis

THE GREAT ONES

OWEN DAVIDSON with C. M. JONES

PELHAM BOOKS

First published in Great Britain by
PELHAM BOOKS LTD
52 Bedford Square
London, W.C.1
1970

7207 0380 8

Set and printed in Great Britain by
Tonbridge Printers Ltd, Peach Hall Works, Tonbridge, Kent
in Baskerville eleven on thirteen point on paper supplied by
P. F. Bingham Ltd, and bound by James Burn
at Esher, Surrey

Contents

ACKNOWLEDGEMENTS

The author's thanks are due to the following, whose pictures are reproduced in this book:

Press Association: 1, 7, 10
C. M. Jones: 2, 3, 13
Central Press Photos: 5, 12
E. Trim & Co.: 4, 6
E. D. Lacey: 8, 11, 14
Le-Roye Productions Ltd.: 9

Illustrations

1: The Early Greats

Everything, so most people believe, has to begin somewhere and any roll of the tennis greats must conform to the pattern. So this story must evolve from the day when Spencer Gore, an Old Harrovian and rackets player of some repute, read that a championship of lawn tennis would be held at the All-England Lawn Tennis & Croquet Club, Worple Road, Wimbledon from 9th to 12th July, 1877 with a delay during the annual Eton and Harrow cricket match; in fact, the first final was played on Thursday, 19th July, 1877, Gore beating W. C. Marshall 6 – 1, 6 – 2, 6 – 4.

Gifted with a natural genius for all games, Gore was extremely mobile, strong, long of reach and original in his thinking.

There remains a widespread belief that in the earliest days of tennis everyone remained at the back of the court, there patting the ball back and back while patiently waiting for the other man to miss. Indeed, there was a period when this became the fashion, but Gore was naturally high in the human 'pecking order'. Not for him such a negative attitude.

Instead, he attacked his opponents from so near a position to the net that a great controversy arose concerning the legality of playing the ball before it actually crossed the net.

Indeed the rule was changed, so Gore must go down as the game's first innovator.

The history of tennis, like war, shows that defences arise to baffle attacks, in turn surrendering to new forms of attack before acquiring new, subtler facets which again put defences on top . . . And so, ad infinitum.

Gore's Nemesis arose twelve short months later when P. F. Hadow, seeing a long legged, gangling man hanging over the net in eager anticipation of a fast, low passing shot, quietly lobbed the ball over his head so it fell near the baseline, sending Gore hustling back in chase and to defeat.

There followed an era of patball before two questioning, experimenting brothers from Cheltenham, William and Ernest Renshaw, developed such all-round strength that they dominated Wimbledon for nine years until the coming of the Baddeley twins, Wilfred and Herbert. Wilfred won Wimbledon three times, changing over the years from a basically steady player to one of great agility and imaginative attack.

Wilfred's reign might have lasted longer but for the arrival of another set of brothers, Reginald Francis and Hugh Lawrence Doherty. There are men alive who saw the Dohertys in action and who have also watched Rod Laver. Clearly, such men were but children in the Doherty era but not such children that their judgment is completely fallible. Thus those who assert that the Dohertys were potentially, if not actually, the equals of present-day stars cannot be completely disregarded.

Factually, Lance Tingay produced in the official British magazine *Lawn Tennis* a 'tennis tree' showing how Gore, the 1877 champion, could be judged better than Rod Laver. The tree runs : Spencer Gore at Wimbledon, 1877, beat W. Marshall who, at Wimbledon 1877, beat L. Erskine who, at Wimbledon 1878, beat W. J. Hamilton who, at Wimbledon 1890, beat J. Pim who, at Wimbledon 1894, beat W. Baddeley who, at Wimbledon 1897, beat H. L. Doherty who, in 1903 U.S. Championships, beat W. A. Larned who, in 1911 U.S. Championships, beat M. McLoughlin who, in 1915 U.S. Championships, beat F. T. Hunter who, in 1928 U.S. Championships, beat J. H. Crawford who, in 1935 Australian Championships, beat A. K. Quist who, in 1947 Australian Hard Court Championships, beat F. A. Sedgman who, in 1960 at Wembley, beat A. Olmedo who, in 1959 in the Wimbledon final, beat R. Laver.

Though such a tree cannot be taken too seriously or literally, it does serve as a reminder that evolution in all things is considerably slower than anarchists and revolutionaries wish or even believe.

Elegant, socially acceptable and highly talented, the Dohertys were, almost surely, the bridge between the older, defensively orientated methods of the nineteenth century beginnings and the powerful, aggressive tactics of today. Strong and beautiful timers of the ball, they possessed gracefully flowing strokes which enabled them to develop greater power than most, maybe all, of their predecessors. Ill-health brought them down eventually, their positions as tennis leaders and public favourites going to Antony Wilding, a New Zealander and, like the Dohertys, a Cambridge University undergraduate and graduate.

Handsome, sensitive and immensely tenacious, Wilding was, deservedly, the 'rave' of the pre-World War I tennis world, during which time he won Wimbledon four years in succession, losing in 1914 to Norman, later Sir Norman, Brookes, a giant who bestrode Australia as player and administrator for 50 abundantly fruitful years.

The friend of literally thousands of players over those years, Brookes served as a wonderful bridge between the past and the future, retaining his form as a player until 1924 when, at the age of 47, he met and beat over five sets at Wimbledon Francis T. Hunter, an American ranked high among the world's top ten and the long-time partner of Bill Tilden.

Whether or not improved communications have been of benefit to humanity may be debatable but the 1914-1918 holocaust brought about immense advances in that field. This, in parallel with universal human need to forget the horrors just over, set up a situation in which leading performers in any sphere of entertainment could readily acquire world fame.

Tilden, like his female contemporary Suzanne Lenglen, exuded the flair, exuberance, provocativeness and general star quality for which the war-strained western world was waiting.

Thus the stage was set for the first of the many all-time tennis 'greats' who have, ever since, inexorably piloted the game to greater heights of popularity. No one could have pioneered better than Tilden.

2: 'Big Bill' Tilden

'Mr Tennis' – the nickname sometimes applied to William Tatem 'Big Bill' Tilden – is thought by many to be the greatest player ever. He had an avid interest in the game, but it never dominated him. Author and playwright, actor and producer, he also enjoyed bridge and music, and recalls the thrill he had when Melba, aunt of his rival Gerald Patterson, recognised him at a London party saying 'You're Gerald's friend, the Blue Grizzly' – a reference to his outsize pullover which caused so much Press comment and delighted the cartoonists.

Born in Philadelphia on 10th February, 1893, nature designed Tilden for efficiency on a tennis court, endowing him with a tall streamlined physique and immense stamina. His slow graceful movements and pleasing, somewhat enigmatic smile led many people to liken him to film star Herbert Marshall, though Tilden considered Marshall looked more like his dead brother (also named Herbert).

His tennis equipment included a tremendous service timed at 124 miles per hour, the best forehand in the world, and a beautifully executed backhand. Allied to these attributes were superb strategy, determination and uncanny anticipation.

His racket was very light – many women players use a heavier one. In 1922 an operation removed the top of one finger; he played even better after it!

A born showman, Tilden had remarkable mannerisms on court, and was equally eccentric in private. Driving a car at an ordinary pace bored him; life had to be vital, energetic, dynamic. A chain smoker, who drank very little, Tilden's outspoken comments when upset alienated a public once drawn by his youthful attractiveness. Nevertheless he possessed many sincere friends

12

who realised that genius needs an outlet and that the American complained only when he felt justified in so doing.

In doubles Tilden always played a glorified single. However, he won many international doubles titles although one critic, describing his double play, declared 'He (Tilden) parked his intelligence outside the stadium,' much to the latter's amusement.

At the age of seven he won his first cup, defeating 'my hated rival, 6 – 0, 0 – 6, 19 – 17'. In the First World War, despite his physique, Tilden was only accepted in the Pay Corps – from which he was granted leave of absence for the 1918 American Championships, in which he reached the singles final, there to lose to R. L. Murray in three sets.

William Johnston was then America's foremost player and in 1919 he and Tilden started a long series of matches which were always packed with incident. In their first encounter flying ants invaded the court and play was postponed an hour. They next met in the U.S. final and Johnston, volleying all Tilden's backhand drives easily, won 6 – 4, 6 – 4, 6 – 3. This defeat made the loser concentrate so hard on this weakness that he developed one of the best backhands of all time. Secure either in attack or defence, his driving on the run has never been equalled.

America invaded Europe in 1920. Patterson was champion and Johnston favourite for the singles, but Tilden's personality stole the limelight, even rivalling Mlle Lenglen for box-office appeal.

When Johnston lost unexpectedly to Parke, Tilden's path to the final was cleared and, before a record crowd, he dethroned Patterson confidently. After toying with the opening set, Tilden attacked the Australian's backhand so cleverly that there was no doubt of the outcome. He won 4 – 6, 6 – 2, 6 – 3, 6 – 4, and immediately refused $25,000 to turn professional.

The tennis world eagerly awaited another Tilden-Johnston duel and in the American singles final of 1920 this was gratified dramatically, Tilden overcoming his rival 6 – 1, 1 – 6, 7 – 5, 5 – 7, 6 – 3, after losing three match points in the fourth set. Rain and an air crash before the gaze of horrified thousands upset play. Johnston's strength eventually failed against ceaseless pressure and he was assisted off court. Tilden's supremacy was complete when he and Johnston wrested the Davis Cup from Australia in December and 'little and big Bill' returned home like conquering heroes.

Early in 1921, however, the champion was struck down by illness and refused the offer of a European tour. At a party soon after, Tilden met President Harding, whom he greatly admired, and the latter persuaded him to change his mind.

Throughout this tour Tilden was a sick man. When he landed in Europe he was covered in boils, and for the week before Wimbledon he rested in a nursing home. His opponent in an amazing final was his friend, little Brian Norton of South Africa, who soon led 6 – 4, 6 – 2. Then Norton made no effort and lost the next two sets 6 – 1, 6 – 0. In the final set he sprang to life, led 5 – 4 and reached match point twice. On the first Tilden drove deep and, believing the ball was going out, ran up to congratulate Norton, but he, thinking Tilden was rushing the net, panicked and netted the return. The next Tilden saved with an ace and he went on to secure the set 7 – 5. It was said that Norton, who possessed Tilden's own hero-worship complex, disliked defeating a sick man. Tilden's state of health was such that he fainted in the dressing room after the match.

Although Tilden regained his health and swept the board at Forest Hills in 1921, his popularity was diminishing in America. Tilden did not mind, for he commanded attention if not affection. His various protégés and his insistence on partnering them in international championships irritated the authorities, who also insisted that Tilden was infringing the always tricky borders of amateurism by his tennis articles. People preferred little Johnston, but no press antagonism could alter the warmth of the friendship between the two 'Bills'.

Little Bill had started the 1922 season brilliantly and at Forest Hills he again challenged Tilden in the final. This meeting was of vital importance to both men; whoever triumphed gained permanent possession of the famous trophy as both had registered two victories. Amidst rising excitement Johnston's volleying won the first two sets. Never robust, he had to forfeit the third but, refreshed after the interval, he led 3 – 0, 40 – 30 on Tilden's service in the fourth. Hitting another deep volley into Tilden's backhand corner, he advanced confidently to the net. A pair of long legs streaked desperately across court and from the farthest corner Tilden raised a perfect diagonal lob that just cleared Johnston's upraised racket. The latter, demoralised, lost six games running, and Tilden cleverly increased his presence, to win the final set and match 4 – 6, 3 – 6, 6 – 2, 6 – 3, 6 – 4 from a weary opponent. Afterwards Johnston told his conqueror 'If I can't have the cup myself, I would prefer you of all men to have it.'

Several critics openly admitted they would prefer Johnston as champion, and when he triumphed at Wimbledon in 1923 hopes were widely expressed for an upset at Forest Hills. But a dominant Tilden, after defeating Norton without removing his sweater, smoothly countered Johnston's attack entirely from the baseline, winning 6 – 4, 6 – 1, 6 – 4, thus completely establishing himself as the world's leading player.

By 1924 the Tilden-Richards battle was widely acknowledged. So when the latter, volleying as one inspired, held Tilden to two sets all in the American semi-final he earned rapturous applause. Heat and tension were terrific when Richards double-faulted to give his rival a 4 – 2 lead in the final set after the Philadelphian had demanded a let, declaring a ball-boy had disturbed him. Pouring iced water over his head, Tilden then served enough aces to win 4 – 6, 6 – 2, 8 – 6, 4 – 6, 6 – 4. Richards collapsed but was immediately awarded Davis Cup colours.

The holder retained his title, beating Johnston 6 – 1, 9 – 7, 6 – 2. He crashed through the first set; brilliant backhand passing shots saved the second; and in the third he hit Johnston off the court, losing only three points in the last three games. Experts agree that this was Tilden's greatest performance.

The Philadelphian at 32 was now at his peak; nevertheless, on his horizon, clouds were gathering. France was determined to capture the Davis Cup, and her apostle was young Lacoste, who realised the only way to defeat Tilden was by stonewalling defence and the ability to steadily return fiery services and drives. This, with Gothic thoroughness, he set out to accomplish.

But not even France could prevent another Tilden-Johnston final in 1925. To win meant another permanent trophy for Tilden, and win he did 4 – 6, 11 – 9, 6 – 3, 4 – 6, 6 – 3, surviving a critical 42-minute second set in which Johnston led 9 – 8, 40 – love. History had seen another cup disappear from the tennis scene and the last of a series of unforgettable battles.

Spectators who were overjoyed in 1924 by the prospect of Tilden losing to 'Vinnie' Richards did not cheer in the Davis Cup final of 1925 when they saw their champion fighting desperately against an even younger man – Lacoste. In their first meeting Tilden had to save four match points before surviving 3 – 6, 10 – 12, 8 – 6, 7 – 5, 6 – 2.

American officials were now becoming worried; probably Tilden himself was worried. Lacoste had not defended his Wimbledon title in 1926 in order to husband his strength and, in the Davis Cup challenge round of that year after Tilden had crushed Borotra and the cup was safe, the Philadelphian suffered his first defeat in important singles since 1920. He lost to Lacoste 4 – 6, 6 – 4, 8 – 6, 8 – 6. Forest Hills provided greater shocks, for in the quarter-final, Cochet, volleying marvellously, defeated Tilden 6 – 8, 6 – 1, 6 – 3, 1 – 6, 8 – 6. He had learnt from Lacoste how to block Tilden's services and he gained speed from his opponent's speed. In the final Lacoste defeated Borotra, to sound the end of an era.

At this time, Suzanne Lenglen and Vincent Richards turned professional. Mr C. C. (Cash & Carry) Pyle, a sports promoter, offered Tilden 25,000 dollars to join them. The Philadelphian, keen on a tennis come-back, refused. The offer was doubled and again rejected. Tilden describes the last interview – Mr Pyle rose and said, 'Mr Tilden, I think you are a damned fool.' I (Tilden) replied, 'Mr Pyle, I think you are probably right.'

Stimulated by defeat, Tilden and his friend Hunter invaded Europe in 1927. He gained a three-set revenge on Cochet in the French semi-final; and in the final failed by one point only, losing to Lacoste 6 – 4, 4 – 6, 5 – 7, 6 – 3, 11 – 9 after three hours' play. Every rally was fought desperately, both men employing every shot and angle. At 9 – 8 in the fifth set Tilden reached match point and hurtled down an apparent ace but Cochet, on the line, declared it was a fault. Another match point, Lacoste served, and eventually his steadiness prevailed amidst unparalleled pandemonium.

Although no longer invincible, Tilden was still a greater draw than the 'Musketeers' at Wimbledon, and in the semi-final a cheeful confident Philadelphian was hitting Cochet off court to lead 6 – 2, 6 – 4, 5 – 1. And then – Tilden lost 17 points in a row. Moreover, Cochet took the set 7 – 5 and led 4 – 2 in the next. A shaken Tilden pulled up to 4 – all, but when his enemy pocketed this set at 6 – 4 it was evident that the younger man's easy volleying would triumph; and France won the last set 6 – 3 before an astounded Centre Court.

Tilden took his reverse magnificently, asserting that Cochet 'came on'. Nobody has ever solved his defeat, but certainly Cochet, a born opportunist, was more fitted to take advantage of a lapse than anyone else.

Tilden and Hunter won the doubles final from Cochet and Brugnon 1 – 6, 3 – 6, 8 – 6, 6 – 3, 6 – 4; a revenge, for Cochet held two match points in the third set. The Americans also triumphed at Forest Hills, but despite this record the U.S. authorities wished to exclude Hunter from the Davis Cup team. Tilden refused to partner anyone else and after bitter wrangling the authorities agreed.

America's chances looked deceptively good when, after Lacoste beat Johnston, Tilden survived a tense four-set match against Cochet and he and Hunter justified themselves by defeating Borotra and Brugnon. But Tilden had not forgiven the committee over Hunter. He writes 'I was absolutely through after the doubles win. I was nervous. My reserves were used up in bickering.' Certainly, since the ex-champion had to bear the brunt of the French attack, it was not politic to worry him about an obvious choice. On the fatal last day Lacoste's defence and the endless chasing he imposed upon Tilden proved decisive in four sets. National sorrow was full when Cochet overcame an untrained Johnston by the same margin. Tilden and Lacoste sat side by side during the final struggle and the former was the first to congratulate his young friends. Lacoste's supremacy was reaffirmed soon after in the Forest Hills final when he defeated Tilden 11 – 9, 6 – 3, 11 – 9, after saving three set points in the first set and another three in the third.

The Philadelphian did not compete at Paris in 1928, but gave Londoners a pre-Wimbledon thrill by appearing at Queen's. In a wonderful exhibition he captured the singles, forfeiting only seventeen games in thirteen sets. In the championships, Tilden's impeccable length foiled Borotra in four sets in the quarter-final, and on 4th July, Americans flocked to witness the finest encounter that year, a Lacoste-Tilden semi-final. A brilliant Tilden led two sets to one and had a point for 4 – 1 in the fourth set, but Lacoste, although worried, held on somehow, saved that set, and his age was decisive in the final set.

The American Committee threatened to bar Tilden because he had written articles describing the play at Wimbledon. Possibly he did not take them seriously, but bar him they did for the Inter-Zone final against Italy. This did not matter, for America could beat Italy without Tilden, but what about the Challenge Round? The 'Musketeers' begged for Tilden to be reinstated, but officialdom was adamant – Tilden must be shown that he was an ordinary mortal. But this is what he proved he was not. The Committee were in America, the Challenge Round in Paris. So was Tilden, who persuaded his captain to ignore trans-Atlantic fury, and allow him to play.

This piquant situation amused Tilden, who celebrated by gaining a dramatic five-set win over Lacoste. Cochet, however, saved France, beating Tilden 9 – 7, 8 – 6, 6 – 4. Later the Committee banned the Philadelphian for six months but, as usual, he had his own way.

Champing after his enforced rest, Tilden returned to Europe in 1929. He met, for the last time, a grim Lacoste in the French semi-final. Missing nothing, and out to revenge his 1928 defeat, Lacoste led 6 – 1, 6 – 0, 5 – 3. With his back to the wall Tilden fought back and won the next four games, but although Lacoste never regained his early mastery, he won the fourth set 6 – 3.

Ill-health prevented Lacoste from defending at Wimbledon, and Tilden's supporters considered he had a good chance but he failed against Cochet in a semi-final that lacked the drama of 1927. Standing well into the American's cannon-balls, even hitting winners off them, and making faultlessly timed, decisive volleying campaigns, Cochet led 6 – 4, 6 – 1, 5 – 1.

As against Lacoste in Paris, Tilden played his desperate best and took four games but his opponent resumed his stranglehold and won 7 – 5.

About this time the theory of the Cochet 'hoodoo' developed; Cochet appeared to have such a complete answer to Tilden's game that the latter was supposed to consider himself beaten before going on court.

One important contribution to Tilden's defeats by Cochet and Lacoste, both of whom were many years his junior, was his inability to drive his fiercest over five sets, and the consequent introduction of cut shots into his attack.

In America Cochet did not defend, and Tilden regained his lost title, proving to be still well ahead of his countrymen. He defeated in turn Van Ryn, Doeg, Shields and Hunter.

Tilden's last, and most strenuous, season in amateur tennis came in 1930. Possibly no man has played so much tennis in one year. He entered for all the Riviera championships and, if programmes were held up, would be fighting out the finals of one tournament while getting through the preliminary rounds of the next. Cochet returned from a Far Eastern tour out of form and was forbidden by his authorities to play singles lest Tilden should break the 'Cochet hoodoo'. So Tilden made almost a clean sweep of all the singles titles.

On the Riviera Tilden paired up with little Cillie Aussem, of Germany. His coaching so improved her tennis and self-confidence that she won the Wimbledon title the following year. Tilden regarded her as his best 'mixed' partner. She denied the romance that was rumoured, saying that she and Tilden were 'great friends'. Five years later (to quote Tilden) 'Cillie married a young Italian Count, whose name I could never remember, and went to live in Africa'. Despite Tilden's interest in his male protégés, his greatest success came with this young German girl.

They partnered each other in Paris and won the title, defeating Borotra-Miss Ryan and Cochet-Mrs Whittingstall. Tilden's mastery of the lob again overcame Borotra in the singles semi-final. He had a good chance in the final, for he led Cochet by a set and 5 – 3, but he allowed the crowd to upset his concentration and Cochet went on to win 3 – 6, 8 – 6, 6 –3, 6 –1.

Tilden's chance at Wimbledon came when, in a major upset in the quarter-final, Cochet lost to the unseeded American Allison.

Left alone to defend France's six-year supremacy at Wimbledon, Borotra – determined to win – fought Tilden – equally determined to make a come-back – in a semi-final that was virtually the final and one of the Centre Court's greatest dramas.

Borotra, six years younger, took the first seven games with a dazzling net attack. Keeping his head, Tilden served aces and won the second set 6 – 4. Another series of net stormings gave Borotra the third set 6 – 4, but this so exhausted him that he threw the fourth to love. He was pushing to towel himself at the net, when Tilden objected declaring Borotra to be delaying deliberately. When asked by the umpire to hurry, Borotra walked off, towel in hand, making a ball-boy run after him. He expected a laugh, and got one. Tilden became furious. 'I fumed' are his own words. Borotra, attacking again, in the final set, led 4 – 2, 30 – 15 on Tilden's service but, unperturbed, Tilden saved the seventh game and took the lead at 5 – 4. A superb smash brought Borotra up to 5 – all, but the next two games went to Tilden.

The final won by Tilden, 6 – 3, 9 – 7, 6 – 4, against a plucky Allison was an anti-climax. His victory was a triumph for a man of 37, and the Centre Court applauded his courage warmly. It also gave him the laugh over his friend Rene Lacoste, who in his *Lacoste on Tennis* published in 1928, stated how interesting it would be to compare the style of the 1930 champion with Tilden.

Back home with an injured leg, Tilden lost to John Doeg in

the American semi-final, $10-8$, $6-3$, $3-6$, $12-10$. He admitted that losing his title again was one of his bitterest blows.

Contrary to general belief Tilden intended to remain an amateur; but he was approached to make a talking picture about tennis. He had been keen to do this for years and the professional contract was signed. In 1931 he opposed Karel Kozeluh, and later Vincent Richards, in a series of matches. Cochet, not now so keen, and a tired Vines followed Tilden's example in 1933. Tilden beat the Frenchman easily and fought Vines, 18 years his junior, on level terms.

One night in Los Angeles, Tilden and Vines played a four-hour match, which the latter won, $6-0$, $5-7$, $21-23$, $6-3$, $6-1$. As they staggered off court, a pretendingly indignant voice shouted at Tilden 'What? No doubles tonight?' It was Charlie Chaplin.

Perry joined the Tilden troupe in 1936. World tour followed world tour. Cochet and Tilden visiting Egypt in 1937 and the Far East in 1938. Vines took up golf and became a plus man but nothing damped Tilden's ardour. During the war, he toured with Budge and Alice Marble, and later became connected with Riggs and Kovacs. In Riggs' opinion Tilden is the greatest player of all time; an opinion shared by nearly every other Wimbledon champion with one notable exception – Borotra, who claims this honour for Budge.

Of Tilden's personal difficulties nothing needs to be said. The world of tennis has expressed its sincere sorrow, Alice Marble referring to him as 'that strange man whom no one understands'. One thing is certain – Tilden in his intolerance of interference made many enemies, while his prowess at tennis must have caused much jealousy. A public figure makes a good shooting target, and as is the case with so many world-famous personalities, the greater the name, the greater the fall.

3: The French Era: Jean Borotra

Such was the strength of Tilden's domination, it took three men to bring about his final downfall.

To rank them is impossible and alphabetical order is the only solution.

First, then, comes Jean Borotra, followed by Henri Cochet and René Lacoste.

A man can become world champion in a sport and yet keep that sport as a secondary consideration in his life. Impossible . . . Look at the Australians . . . Specialisation is absolutely essential . . . These, and a dozen different denials of that statement, will come tumbling into mind, yet one of the most outstanding performers in the history of any sport has proved it to be true.

The man is Jean Borotra, and if anyone doubts that he was the equal of, or better than, the stars of today, let him ponder awhile on a few of these achievements: Six Wimbledon titles, nine American Championship titles, three Australian championship titles (the only three he ever played in), over sixty French titles, sixteen consecutive years in the French Davis Cup team, including the six when France were the winners.

His enormous list of successes would have been even bigger but for one thing. He played only in those tournaments where he could combine business and tennis.

No man, not even an Englishman, has ever captured the British public so completely as the lithe, bounding, dynamic young Basque who made his Wimbledon début way back in 1922.

It was an auspicious year. The new Wimbledon had been officially opened by King George V, unluckily in synchronism with the wettest fortnight in the history of the championships. Daily the rain poured down, and the outside courts went out of commission for days on end. But still crowds flocked in and, as a small reward for their devotion, had their first glimpse of this man who was to hold top place in their affections for more than three decades.

Though immediately popular – the crowds loved his Latin chivalry, obvious pleasure in play, courage, gallantry, and sportsmanship – his first two visits hardly hinted at the fabulous height he would later reach. Beaten by Patterson in the second round, he reached the fifth round in 1923, only to lose in straight sets to Norton.

But at Wimbledon in 1924, in the absence of Tilden and Johnston, Borotra struck his dynamic best. Confident after beating Lacoste for the French Championship, he easily overthrew America's strongest challenger, Vincent Richards, in the quarter-finals, and then thrashed Louis Raymond to make it the first-ever all-French final.

Volleying audaciously and with breathtaking speed, he beat Lacoste 6 – 1, 3 – 6, 6 – 1, 3 – 6, 6 – 4, to begin six years of glorious French domination over these championships.

'Mesdames et Messieurs, Jean Borotra est arrivé!' And how!

A brilliant man – he holds degrees in both engineering and law, and in his twenties was a director of an industrial organisation with branches in twenty-five countries – Borotra early made headlines with his endless dashes by air from Paris to Wimbledon, during which he frequently changed into his tennis clothes.

Sandwiched in between, somehow, anyhow, were meetings, conferences, interviews, and these often continued whilst he changed in the dressing-room. Indeed, on one memorable occasion he dealt with two hard-headed American business men from the bath in which he was relaxing after beating Lacoste in the Wimbledon singles semi-final.

Perhaps his philosophy of life explains his ceaseless energy. 'Life for me would be a poor thing with only one aim. Suppose one has the ambition to be a world champion in sport. Either one succeeds or one doesn't. If one does, it cannot last for ever.

Eventually a successor comes along. So whether or not one reaches the top, disappointment or heart-break must be somewhere along the route. But if one has other interests, one can immediately concentrate on them, forget about the failure or fall down, and consequently go through life with much greater pleasure. Life is nothing without variety.' That was how he once summed it up.

His attendance at a business lunch immediately before his 1927 Wimbledon final with Cochet, proved beyond question that these were no empty words.

Borotra's zest for action, speed and variety stood out on court. With his endless stock of berets, vivid and valiant character, and brilliant buoyancy, he quickly became the cartoonist's perfect model, though all of them complained how difficult he was to caricature.

His tennis, dynamic and unorthodox, flourished on a net attack the like of which may never again be seen. His volleys, even in the 1950s, still normally ended the rally immediately and his bounds carried him so rapidly from one side-line to the other that his hapless victims must have attributed to him the magic of ubiquity.

Often they resorted in desperation to lobbing, but Borotra running backwards was faster than many men of half his age running forward. Only lobbing campaigns executed with the timing and accuracy of a Lacoste or Tilden stood any hope of success.

An apparently moderate service was, in fact, better than good because of its intelligent integration with his net play, and for ten years was as difficult to break as the more spectacular cannon-balls of the Americans. A fair forehand, moderate backhand, plus uncanny intelligence and tactical sense, made up the rest of his game.

The 1927 Wimbledon semi-final illustrates his intelligence. Playing Lacoste of the perfect backhand, he quickly spotted an unusual backhand weakness, and equally quickly left it severely alone. Swapping serves for the first two sets he attacked the backhand on two only of Lacoste's service games, obtaining a break each time. For the next two sets he held back, assiduously feeding Lacoste's forehand and lulling him into a false sense of security.

With the opening of the fifth set the crowd's apparently 'dead' hero sprang suddenly to life, unleashed an all-out attack on a backhand insufficiently practised to be in any certain groove and in a twinkling reached the final 6 – 4, 6 – 3, 1 – 6, 1 – 6, 6 – 2.

No one appreciated his tactics more than Lacoste, who said : 'I was filled with admiration for his intelligence.'

Borotra's nervous energy is in keeping with his intelligence, and has bewildered many an opponent.

Apparently exhausted after two fast sets, Borotra has often staggered around the baseline for two more sets and looked thoroughly beaten. But concentration, indomitable will to win, knowledge of when and where to apply pressure or withdraw, enormous courage, and an intense sense of the dramatic have supplied him with an apparently never-ending supply of nervous energy in crisis after crisis during his thirty years of international play, frequently to the chagrin of his opponents.

His matches in the American National singles championship of 1926 were classics of this kind. Down two sets to one against Richards, Borotra revived to win 3 – 6, 6 – 4, 4 – 6, 8 – 6, 6 – 2. Listless, apparently finished, after Johnston had won the first two sets 6 – 3, 6 – 4, he rallied to win the next three 6 – 3, 6 – 4, 8 – 6.

This brought bitter criticism from Tilden who commented acidly, 'Borotra, apparently dying on his feet – staggering – gasping – sitting on the sand box by the umpire's chair . . . then launched a net attack that swept Johnson out of the tournament.'

How ironic, that he, who had so often called on such reserves of nervous energy himself should have failed to recognise in Borotra those self-same qualities of courage and will-to-win, mentally overcoming genuine physical exhaustion.

Such physical exhaustion was in no way the result of neglect, for he is exemplary in his temperance and exercised as assiduously in 1969 as in his first years at Wimbledon. The sheer speed of his play taxed him to limits which only the strongest spiritual strengths could overcome but it is those very spiritual strengths which make the Borotras of this world.

Magnificent in singles, Borotra at times excelled in doubles, especially mixed, in which his daring poachings and electrifying bounds transfixed in turn all the leading women of the day.

With Borotra at the net, return of service became a constant struggle to avoid the apparently telescopic racket in his hand.

Winning at Wimbledon with Lacoste in 1925, he paired there with Brugnon for the first time in 1932, and reached his acrobatic best whilst beating Allison and Van Ryn in the semi-final.

Though they had won the title in 1929 and 1930, the Americans were unable to take a set. In one rally Borotra landed on the parapet which surrounds the centre court, sat there watching Brugnon defend heroically for several shots and then, spotting an opening, rushed back on to hit a breathtaking winner.

In the final they beat Perry and Hughes 7 – 5 in the fifth set, Borotra again playing brilliantly, and also stimulating Brugnon in his unsteady periods by whispering victoire into his ear. They retained their title the following year.

In 1932 Vines smashed his way through Maier, Crawford and Austin for the loss of only a handful of games to capture the Wimbledon singles with probably the finest tennis ever played anywhere.

Borotra, pleading that he was too old, appealed to the French selection committee to play Boussus in singles, and to let him partner Brugnon in the doubles. Eventually, under pressure, Borotra agreed to play singles – 'For France' – but it had to be the last time.

Opposing Vines in the opening rubber, the grimly concentrating Borotra handled the cannon-ball services beautifully (they were timed at 128 m.p.h., 8 m.p.h. faster than Gonzales' fastest) and before an unbelieving but delirious crowd took the first two sets 6 – 4, 6 – 2.

Adjusting himself to Borotra's clever slowing-down tactics,

Vines crashed home the third set 6 – 3 and appeared poised for victory.

Courageously switching to an all-or-nothing net attack, the rapidly tiring Borotra fought his way to 5 – 4 and, in conditions of near hysteria, caused the biggest surprise of a decade by taking the match in the tenth game.

As a reward for their stupendous play, both men were afterwards introduced to the French President.

Two days later Borotra wrote 'finis' to a glorious Davis Cup singles record by defeating Allison in the deciding rubber of the Challenge Round, after Allison had held match point.

But if he was finished with Davis Cup singles, he certainly wasn't with play on covered courts. The fast and accurate bounce of the ball on wood, the absence of sun and wind, and the security of the foothold made him well-nigh unplayable.

Covered Court champion of Britain and France eleven times each, the last time at Queen's in 1949, he added one more championship to his total by winning the 1952 French mixed doubles with Jean Rinkel from the 1953 and 1955 Wimbledon singles runner-up, Kurt Nielsen and the French number one, Nellie Adamson.

His final appearance in singles at Wimbledon inevitably became dramatic. Entering only to gain practice for doubles, he won from Henkel, the German number two, in five sets, lost a thriller with Menzel 11 – 9 in the fifth set, and was immediately denounced by a French critic for his refusal to play Davis Cup singles.

Borotra, D'Artagnan to his finger-tips, immediately issued a challenge – they would fight a duel. Lacoste was appointed his second but the quarrel simmered down and was forgotten.

On 25th July, 1937, Borotra married Mme Edouard Barrachin, half-sister of golf champion John de Forest.

Marriage, business and an Alpine accident restricted his tennis, but he partnered Helen Moody at Wimbledon in 1938, losing in the quarter-final to Budge and Alice Marble. Spectators were surprised to see America's 'poker-face' so amused by Borotra's antics that she often gave way to hilarious merriment.

The last 'Musketeers' still retained their skill, for in Paris in 1939 Borotra and Brugnon, after beating the top Americans, Cooke and Riggs, in three sets, only lost the final, 10 – 8 in the fifth set, to McNeill and Harris, the winners saving three match points. The Frenchmen reached the Wimbledon semi-final where Cooke and Riggs had their revenge in four sets.

In 1940 he was appointed High Commissioner of Sport by the Vichy Government. His headquarters became a secret centre of resistance, and in 1943 when General Giraud fled to North Africa, Borotra tried to escape. He was captured by the Nazis and imprisoned.

In 1946 feelings were still high against Vichy, and Borotra's entry for Wimbledon was refused. In 1947, twenty-five years after his first Davis Cup match, Borotra and Petra lost to Drobny and Cernik, 10 – 8, 14 – 12, 6 – 3.

That year he won the French covered court title beating Bergelin and Johannson; while, with Marcel Bernard, Borotra won the U.S. covered court doubles in 1948.

Peace was restored in 1948, and, with Mme Boegner and Brugnon, Borotra returned to Wimbledon. He received a tremendous ovation, for although he no longer wore his beret, everything that the Centre Court had grown to love, and to laugh at, was still there.

These Wimbledon appearances are only for old times' sake. Not so at Queen's Club, where he again won the covered courts championship in 1948 – a great achievement, generously applauded by the 1,000 spectators who rose to their feet to acclaim him. Borotra retained the title in 1949, but lost in the semi-final to G. L. Paish in 1950.

Jean Borotra was born in Biarritz on 13th August, 1898. He has played more Davis Cup tennis than any other Frenchman, and has appeared in partnership with Brugnon alone on more than 100 occasions.

The hero of the ball boys, Borotra has added to tennis a chronicle of courtesy and charm.

4: The French Era:
Henri Cochet

Borotra had his beret . . . Donald Budge had a blazing head
. . . Suzanne had hysterics. Most champions claim some
characteristic, so Cochet cultivated nonchalance. The word
became his copyright and is invariably used to describe his
ambling, self-contained attitude.

The greatest genius of the 'Musketeers' – some say, of all time
– he replaced Lacoste's industry by indolence. Where Borotra
galloped, Cochet glided – and his trick of seemingly invisible
movement remains unique.

Born in 1901, Henri Cochet's tennis started at the age of
seven, when 'the game became a passion with me'. His effortless
improvised wizardry has been called 'errand boy tennis' – biting
retorts by a quick brain. A mild service was offset by the deadliest
smash executed by a small man. When roused, Cochet produced
wonder backhands, but it was his magnificent forehand that
prepared his net attack.

Wandering casually into 'no-man's land,' Cochet would hit
volleys and half volleys off his very toes. Placed down the line or
almost parallel to the net, these exquisite shots were executed
with easy abandon.

Naturally lazy, no other champion has recovered so often from
seemingly hopeless positions. Before a Davis Cup final, Cochet
forgot tennis for a country holiday. Then, inspired by excitement, he was transformed.

Military champion of France in 1921, Cochet hit the headlines next year, winning the French singles and three titles in the

'World's Hard Court' championships. At Wimbledon he lost the third round 6 – 3, 6 – 0, 6 – 4 to Joe Anderson.

At his second Wimbledon, in 1925, Cochet started his battles against Borotra, losing the semi-final 5 – 7, 8 – 6, 6 – 4, 6 – 1. Next year Borotra duplicated this feat 2 – 6, 7 – 5, 2 – 6, 6 – 3, 7 – 5. This colourful encounter drew from Bunny Austin 'A poor shot would have been welcomed!'

In America, Cochet scored his greatest win yet, dramatically dethroning Tilden (champion since 1920) 6 – 8, 6 – 1, 6 – 3, 1 – 6, 8 – 6. The American admitted 'crying off' as Cochet's last volley eluded him. In the semi-final, Lacoste's persistence overcame Cochet 3 – 6, 6 – 4, 4 – 6, 8 – 6, 6 – 2. All fashionable Paris turned out for the Cochet-Tilden semi-final of 1927. By a surprise attack on Cochet's forehand, Tilden was avenged 9 – 7, 6 – 3, 6 – 2.

Thanks to Cochet 1927 is considered the most remarkable Wimbledon ever. Down two sets to Frank Hunter, Cochet started that paralysing glide forward. Hunter sent for his friend, Tilden. Together they collected only seven more games.

Tilden's cyclone hitting led Cochet by two sets and 5 – 1. Suddenly Cochet stiffened – the cannon-balls flew back – and the bewildered Centre Court saw him pocket seventeen successive points and the set, 7 – 5. Becoming a brick wall against which the harassed American beat helplessly, Cochet sailed home 2 – 6, 4 – 6, 7 – 5, 6 – 4, 6 – 3.

Even more perilous was his plight in the final with Borotra (holder) leading 5 – 2 in the fifth set. Gaily confident, Cochet saved six match points, one by a volley Borotra and many spectators considered a double hit. But the umpire decided otherwise, and Destiny awarded Cochet the title 4 – 6, 4 – 6, 6 – 3, 6 – 4, 7 – 5.

Paris 1928 revealed a superhuman Cochet. His volleying, to quote Helen Wills, was 'invincible'. His victims included Sydney Wood, Hunter, Borotra, Lacoste.

But at Wimbledon Cochet lost a somewhat listless final to Lacoste 6 – 1, 4 – 6, 6 – 4, 6 – 2. Lacoste's mechanical passes frequently clipped the lines. By beating Tilden 9 – 7, 8 – 6, 6 – 4 in the Davis Cup and winning the U.S. title, Cochet was, however, ranked No. 1 for 1928 – a position he retained four years.

Pantomime helped to defeat Cochet in the French semi-final in 1929. Despite the terrific tempo, Borotra, falling, decided to roll over on his face. Rising, he ejected a pebble from his mouth – and then, another. Repeated bursts of laughter startled Cochet who miss-hit two returns. Enraged, he lost touch and title to the tune of 6 – 3, 5 – 7, 7 – 5, 5 – 7, 6 – 4.

Wimbledon provided revenge – 'Never did I feel so sure of myself.' This was apparent when, taking every shot on the rise, he dismissed Tilden 6 – 4, 6 – 3, 7 – 5.

In the final, Cochet, deadly on drive and volley, outpaced even the nimble Borotra. The Basque, constantly foot-faulting, surrendered 6 – 4, 6 – 3, 6 – 4.

Cochet was popularly supposed to 'mesmerise' Tilden. When he beat his rival 3 – 6, 8 – 6, 6 – 3, 6 – 1 in the French final of 1930, no other player was considered at Wimbledon. Cochet's quarter-final defeat (6 – 4, 6 – 4, 6 – 3) by unseeded Wilmer Allison was, therefore, a world surprise. Shaking his head sadly and clapping his thigh to stir himself, the Frenchman's standard was definitely 'sub Cochet' but he declared 'No bad luck. Allison won by marvellous tennis.'

Influenza and malaria prevented Cochet defending in Paris in 1931. Convalescent at Wimbledon, the first round proved fatal, Cochet losing 6 – 1, 6 – 3, 6 – 2 to base-liner Nigel Sharpe.

But the Davis Cup re-created the master touch. To beat Austin and Perry, Cochet played such truly amazing tennis that nobody doubted his world superiority. As France's mainstay, Cocket refused a wonderful professional offer from Tilden.

Despite U.S. boosting of a new Tilden (Ellsworth Vines), all seemed well in that spring of 1932 when Cochet swept the board in Paris. Something, however, went wrong at Wimbledon, where the second round saw him beaten by Ian Collins 6 – 2, 8 – 6, 0 – 6, 6 – 3.

Although not then realised, this was the first sign of a declining Cochet. He timed the alarm as usual for the third set and played dazzling tennis but its warning failed to rouse him again in the fourth.

France had already retained the Davis Cup when Vines beat Cochet 4 – 6, 0 – 6, 7 – 5, 8 – 6, 6 – 2. To avenge his first Davis Cup loss since 1927, Cochet invaded America.

After four brilliant sets between Cochet and Allison, the umpire stopped the U.S. semi-final owing to bad light. Cochet protested – it might mean playing twice on one day. Overruled, he beat Allison next morning 6 – 1, 10 – 12, 4 – 6, 6 – 3, 7 – 5.

Although Vines only aced Cochet six times, his deep crashing drives, foiling Cochet's net onslaught, really won the final 6 – 4, 6 – 4, 6 – 4. Interviewed, Cochet admitted fatigue before starting, due to playing twice.

Early in 1933, Cochet, toying with the idea of joining Tilden, was forbidden to make a film combining tennis and romance. In the French final, after a wonderful first set, Cochet's stimulus vanished and he lost to Jack Crawford 8 – 6, 6 – 1, 6 – 3.

About this reverse Vines said 'Cochet knows he is a super player – competition has lost its flavour'. A record Wimbledon crowd witnessed the Vines-Cochet semi-final. Cochet disappointed his countless supporters – his backhand was uncertain and Vines stormed through the fourth set (6 – 2, 8 – 6, 3 – 6, 6 – 1).

In the best Davis Cup match of 1933 Cochet came back to rarified heights beating Austin (recent victor over Vines and Allison) 5 – 7, 6 – 4, 4 – 6, 6 – 4, 6 – 4. After his heart had been pronounced fit during the interval, Cochet's breathtaking volleys saved the final set from 2 – 4 down. Sending a ball sky-high, Cochet wrung Austin's hand – and collapsed. Cheers changed to consternation as he left the court on a stretcher.

Soon after occurred the 'Cochet week'. After ceaseless rumours that kept Paris guessing for six days Cochet signed up with Tilden. In World War Two Cochet did legion service visiting prisoners-of-war. Reinstated as amateur, he beat Petra eight

'Big Bill' Tilden in 1921

Henri Cochet (*left*) and
Jean Borotra at
Wimbledon, 1927

René Lacoste (*right*)
with S. B. Wood

times in 1943. French covered court champion in 1945, Cochet was still able to hold his own with anybody for three sets.

To Tilden, Cochet was 'The greatest player the world has ever seen'. Certainly no champion has given his supporters more thrills or his opponents more shocks than this gay-minded little man from Lyons.

5: The French Era: René Lacoste

It was on an August morning in 1923 that the French Davis Cup captain saw his youngest player gazing into a New York shop window.

This pale dark youth of medium height was absorbed by a magnificent toy crocodile. Asked if he would like it, Jean René Lacoste joyfully agreed – it became his emblem and he wore a crocodile badge on his shirt. Paris affectionately named him 'Monsier le Crocodile'.

Referring to France's Davis Cup win in 1927, Lacoste spoke of Pierre Gillou's leadership, and the spirit of the 'Musketeers'. Modest and self-effacing, he always omitted his tactical genius that learned how to overthrow Tilden, backbone of American tennis.

Lacoste might be called the Captain of Industry in Tennis. Practice anywhere, anyhow, even against a cushion if no wall were available, perfected a tennis machine. Sometimes he could only be 'heard' at practice – it was too dark to see the player.

Delicate in health, his will was iron, his self-discipline immense. And his tragedy came when, after he achieved his heart's desire and won the Davis Cup for France, Lacoste's health collapsed under the strain, compelling him to retire at 24.

One of the shyest champions, Lacoste's inability to speak English fluently added to his reserve. Nevertheless, his personality was as effective as his more dynamic contemporaries, Borotra and Cochet. Lacoste took his tennis seriously, but his big white cap and solemn expression concealed his enjoyment of the game.

He was happiest when engaged in a life-and-death struggle – and his bitterest enemies were his greatest friends.

Methodical to the last degree, Lacoste was often ragged by his team-mates about his famous notebooks (a dossier of all opponents) but he considered them invaluable, even refusing to sell them for 1,000 dollars.

His concentration was uncanny. Playing Lycett at Wimbledon in 1925 he did not notice the arrival of the Royal Family, which caused 15,000 spectators to rise. Only when he started to serve did Lacoste see Lycett standing motionless on the court.

Heartbreaking in his baseline accuracy, Lacoste often subdued far more versatile opponents. He possessed an impregnable backhand and wonderful management of the lob. The Frenchman seldom had an 'off' day – sometimes a super Tilden or an extra-brilliant Cochet would produce enough winners to overcome Lacoste, but it needed tremendous sustained aggression.

Born on 2nd July, 1905, Lacoste took up tennis to improve his health. He lost his first match at Wimbledon in 1922 to Australian Pat O'Hara Wood. In 1923, however, he was French covered court champion – beating in the quarter-final 'a somewhat sleepy Borotra at 10 o'clock in the morning after a very short night' – and at Wimbledon that summer he reached the fifth round.

Lacoste's first visit to America in 1923, where he lost in the second round to F. T. Hunter (in five sets), drew the comment from Mrs Wightman, famous for her insight, that France had a world-beater.

Borotra beat Lacoste 7 – 5, 6 – 4, 0 – 6, 4 – 6, 6 – 2 in the French final of 1924 and duplicated his victory at Wimbledon a month later.

This final was sharp and short although going to five sets (6 – 1, 3 – 6, 6 – 1, 3 – 6, 6 – 4) – Borotra's volleying, and possibly his stronger personality, turned the tables. Victor and vanquished walked off the court arm-in-arm – France had won!

Only lack of confidence had held Lacoste back, and Borotra forecast his young friend would be next champion. And in 1925 after a stream of perfect lobs over Borotra's racket had given

Lacoste his first French championship in three sets (7 – 5, 6 – 1, 6 – 4) these rivals again met in the Wimbledon final.

Down two sets, Borotra tightened up his errors, and some brilliant volleying gave him the third set. Moreover, he led 4 – 1 in the fourth, but Borotra's footfaults and his own resourcefulness then saved Lacoste, who proved his humanity by joyfully flinging off his cap and rushing to the net to receive Borotra's congratulations. The score was 6 – 3, 6 – 3, 4 – 6, 8 – 6.

Although thrilled by Paris and Wimbledon, Lacoste was still unsatisfied – the Davis Cup lay securely behind the shadow of the American giant, Tilden. Lacoste realised that Tilden (twelve years his senior) needed enormous elbow room for his crushing drives.

He planned therefore to run Tilden up and down court, and provoke errors by medium-paced hitting. These tactics entailed the ability to return a barrage of withering drives and cannonball services – this Lacoste patiently practised to achieve.

In 1925, France reached the Davis Cup final. Lacoste, meeting Tilden for the first time, staggered America by almost succeeding in his campaign. Four times within a point of defeat in the fourth set, Tilden only saved himself by his great courage (4 – 6, 10 – 12, 8 – 6, 7 – 5, 6 – 2).

At Forest Hills, Vincent Richards eased U.S. minds when by a brilliant net attack he beat Lacoste 6 – 4, 6 – 3, 6 – 3 in the quarter-final. But Lacoste's exertions had exhausted him. Soon after he developed congestion of the lung and in the French semi-final of 1926 he failed to win a set from Cochet.

Lacoste now realised that if he were to make any impression on Tilden, he would have to miss Wimbledon. This sacrifice paid a dividend, for although America retained the Davis Cup, Lacoste beat Tilden 4 – 6, 6 – 4, 8 – 6, 8 – 6. This was Tilden's first Davis Cup defeat for six years. To increase Gallic joy, Cochet defeated Tilden in the U.S. singles quarter-final.

Tilden took a line in the Cochet-Lacoste semi-final won by the latter, 3 – 6, 6 – 4, 4 – 6, 8 – 6, 6 – 2. Lacoste then established himself as the world's No. 1 when he became the first Frenchman to win in America. He played superbly to beat

Borotra (conqueror of Richards and Johnston) 6 – 4, 6 – 0,
6 – 4. Borotra led 4 – 2, but a cascade of lobs then escaped the
best smash in tennis and Lacoste won the next ten games.

His defeats nettled Tilden and drew him out of America in
1927. Paris seethed with excitement when he and Lacoste met
in the greatest-ever French final. In the third set Lacoste was
attacked by cramp. Rain and free fights, all of which bothered
Tilden but never Lacoste, marked the final set. At 8 – 7 Tilden
reached match point twice, but Lacoste hung on, and finally
battled through to a desperate finish, 6 – 4, 4 – 6, 5 – 7, 6 – 3,
11 – 9.

Seeded No. 1 and No. 2, they were expected to decorate the
Wimbledon final – yet neither survived the semi-final. Cochet
beat Tilden, and Borotra, his enthusiasm fired because a French
victory was now assured, scored a strategic win over Lacoste,
6 – 4, 6 – 3, 1 – 6, 1 – 6, 6 – 2.

But in September a five-year dream came true. 'A thousand
photographs . . . seems like a fantasy . . . l'Elysee'; thus Lacoste
describes France's Davis Cup win. He took the lion's share of
honour, beating Johnston in three sets and Tilden in four. To
cement French supremacy Lacoste retained the U.S. title, defeating Tilden 11 – 9, 6 – 3, 11 – 9.

Resting in the winter of 1927-28, the Frenchman completed
Lacoste on Tennis, a masterpiece of information; and on 22nd
March, 1928, he demonstrated at the Asnieres Club his tennis
machine, which resembling an anti-aircraft gun, could shoot
balls across court and could lob to a height of fifteen feet.

Cochet's win at Wimbledon in 1927 had greatly increased
his confidence. At Paris in 1928 he beat Hunter and Borotra,
and in the final produced such a pace that Lacoste could only
win one set, 5 – 7, 6 – 3, 6 – 1, 6 – 3.

At Wimbledon, Lacoste survived a critical semi-final against
a brilliant Tilden, who led two sets to one and had a point for
4 – 1 in the fourth. Lacoste's age and scrambling ability,
however, eventually won the match by three sets to two.

These battles finished Lacoste for 1929. He could not defend
his Wimbledon title or the Davis Cup. A year went by and he

married France's golfing star, attractive Simonne de la Thaume. He was Davis Cup captain in 1931, but when Borotra collapsed in his arms after playing Perry, and Vines arrived on the scene, something had to be done to assist Cochet to retain the trophy.

Lacoste accordingly risked his stamina and re-entered tennis in 1932. He sent the crowd mad with delight when he put out Sydney Wood, reigning Wimbledon champion, in the most sensational match of the French championships, 6 – 1, 6 – 0, 3 – 6, 6 – 8, 7 – 5.

But the strain was too great, and Lacoste's concentration was not now so powerful. He lost his next match in four sets to H.G.N. Lee, and could never again play serious tennis.

France now realised with a sigh that her youngest 'Musketeer' could offer her his wonderful brain, but no longer his body. Lacoste remained Davis Cup captain for many years, and was recognised for the kindness he showed to young players.

Today his tennis is a fragrant reminder of the twenties. Lacoste played in wonderful company. He partnered Suzanne at her zenith, he engineered the fall of Tilden. But his greatest love was for France. Glory for Lacoste meant nothing compared to glory for France – and to this end he directed all his skill and stamina.

Yet his interest in tennis never died and in the 1960s he made steel rackets possible and now holds world patents on most of the ever-increasing numbers seen around the world. 1969 saw him become even more deeply immersed, for he was elected to high office among the new group of tennis lovers who were voted in as the controlling force in the French Lawn Tennis Federation.

6: Ellsworth Vines

French domination as a team continued until 1933 when Britain finally wrested the Davis Cup from them. But individual supremacy was overcome earlier than this. Just as they had jointly suppressed one American, Bill Tilden, so it was another American, Ellsworth Vines, who overtook them.

It is not a rarity to see a cannon-ball service on the Wimbledon Centre Court. Many a hard-fought rally has terminated with a withering drive. But no champion has generated such continuous devastating speed over so long a period as Californian H. Ellsworth Vines.

This likeable twenty-two year old, with the gangling Gary Cooper outline, hit Wimbledon in cyclonic fashion in 1932. With a fiery display he power-charged through a star-studded competition, losing only 13 games in the last three matches.

On court, Vines was no Borotra. He looked grim, almost forbidding – until a sudden smile, which screwed up the corners of his eyes, would transform his expression.

Vines had very slow, deliberate movements. He never took to shorts, and often wore a white peaked cap. His 128 miles per hour service, involving slight lift and spin, was a terror to his opponents; and even when he had virtually retired, Vines averaged two aces per game in exhibitions against Donald Budge.

With the ideal position for the waist-high drive, Vines had a murderous forehand and a very good backhand. Controlled speed, plus a marvellous phlegmatic temperament, were the reasons for his amazing successes.

The great Dick Williams, team-mate of Tilden and Johnston, declared Vines was the best thing in U.S. tennis for a decade, after seeing him win the Pacific South-West title in 1930.

Williams proved no mean prophet. In 1931, Vines rose from America's No. 10 to No. 1. Not even Tilden had a better U.S. season. After winning the Clay Court singles, Vines beat John Doeg (American title holder) 10 – 12, 6 – 8, 6 – 3, 8 – 6, 6 – 1 at Seabright; and again in the Longwood Bowl final 4 – 6, 6 – 3, 6 – 3, 3 – 6, 6 – 3.

After he had beaten Shields, Van Ryn and Perry to win at Newport, Vines was top seed at Forest Hills. Calmly cannon-balling, despite an adverse score, Vines beat Perry 4 – 6, 3 – 6, 6 – 4, 6 – 4, 6 – 3 in the semi-final.

Another Vines-Doeg battle was anticipated, but Lott defeated Doeg, and 10,000 spectators saw Vines successfully attack Lott's unorthodoxy in the final to win 7 – 9, 6 – 3, 9 – 7, 7 – 5, after Lott led 5 – 2 in the fourth set.

Two more victories over Perry at Los Angeles and San Francisco completed a great season.

France was now the champion country. But their Davis Cup Committee was perturbed by Vines' exploits. They looked anxiously at Cochet, now over thirty, and even less in-clined to train as in the days when Tilden was his greatest menace.

When an uncertain Vines lost to Hopman at Queen's Club in 1932, French hopes rose. At Wimbledon, Cochet, seeded No. 1, was strongly favoured for the title.

Usually, the holder opens proceedings on the Centre Court. This year, however, Vines was awarded that honour. And, as it happened, he hit the last ball there.

Cochet, again taking things too easily, made one of his sensa-tional early round exits. Vines gave a taste of his power by his quarter-final defeat of the brilliant Spaniard, Maier (conqueror of Borotra) 6 – 2, 6 – 3, 6 – 2.

Even more devastating was his forty-minute victory over Crawford. The Australian's powerful services were hit for winners, while Vines won seven service games for the loss of three points. A measure of his power was that one game yielded four aces. This 6 – 2, 6 – 1, 6 – 3 display on a damp court drew from Cochet, 'Pretty good – wonderful – never seen anything like it.'

Austin's classic tennis had beaten Shields and Satoh. But from 3-all in the final he was powerless against Vines. Demoralised by a series of terrific Californian drives, services and smashes, Austin made little effort to stem the avalanche. Vines won 6–4, 6–2, 6–0 in 45 minutes.

Photographs showed Vines, who was a friend of the Englishman, offering anxious sympathy rather than receiving congratulations!

Excitement mounted in Paris over the impending Cochet-Vines duel in the Davis Cup Challenge Round. But on the opening day, 33-year-old Borotra handled Vines' cannon-balls beautifully. Nursing his reserves, Borotra curbed his net-rushing unless certain of a kill, and urged on by a frenzied crowd defeated Vines 6 – 4, 6 – 2, 3 – 6, 6 – 4.

Although France was victorious, Vines scored a great personal triumph. Dazed by Cochet's wizardry for two sets, Vines then hit out fearlessly. A feast of beautiful tennis followed, but the Californian kept even Cochet from the net, and to the amazement of the crowd – Cochet had not lost a Davis Cup match since 1927 – Vines won 4 – 6, 0 – 6, 7 – 5, 8 – 6, 6 – 2.

To regain his supremacy, Cochet entered the U.S. championship. Vines all but lost his semi-final to Clifford Sutter (conqueror of Austin). Vines' service and temperament prevailed after 75 games (4 – 6, 8 – 10, 12 – 10, 10 – 8, 6 – 1).

In the final, Vines beat Cochet 6 – 4, 6 – 4, 6 – 4. Cochet was unlucky in having to finish his semi-final against Allison that morning, and he was only aced by Vines six times. The match was won by Vines' superb drives which, raising chalk, neutralised Cochet's greatest strength – his ability to glide to the net.

His win made Vines the idol of U.S. tennis. On 1st October, two days after his twenty-first birthday, the Californian was married. He would have done well to have now taken a leaf out of Cochet's book, and rested from tennis – instead, he accompanied an American team on an ill-fated Australian tour.

Vine's only win was at Sydney, where he beat Allison 4 – 6,

6 – 1, 2 – 6, 6 – 4, 7 – 5. In the Victorian final, Crawford, standing into Vines' thunderbolts, triumphed 1 – 6, 6 – 4, 6 – 4, 2 – 6, 6 –4.

In January, 1933, occurred the biggest shock of the tour. This was in the Australian quarter-final, when seventeen-year-old Vivian McGrath defeated a weary and over-played Vines, 6 – 2, 2 – 6, 8 – 6, 7 – 5.

Back in America, Tilden made Vines a tempting professional offer which, according to Tilden, Vines found 'deeply interesting'. These negotiations reached the ears of the U.S. authorities. When Tilden wrote Vines wishing him luck in Europe in 1933, Vines' captain insisted on reading the contents, even declaring he would forbid Vines to play in the Davis Cup, unless he obeyed.

This bickering did not help a jaded Vines at Wimbledon. Nevertheless, before a record semi-final crowd, he beat Cochet 6 – 2, 8 – 6, 3 – 6, 6 – 1. The second set, saved by Vines from 2 – 5, settled the issue. Cochet did wonders at the net, but in the fourth set Vines' lashing drives were untouchable.

Vines, so violent, and Crawford, so classic, provided one hundred minutes of thrills in the final. Crawford yielded first blood to Vines' ace, but the Australian, hugging his baseline, won the long, vital second set. Even Vines' strong serving arm was tiring, and fewer cannon-balls found their mark.

Both men threw a set apiece – and resumed the fight desperately in the fifth. Leading 5 – 4, Crawford suddenly switched to a net attack, Vines, astonished, netted twice to give the Australian a magnificent victory 4 – 6, 11 – 9, 6 – 2, 2 – 6, 6 – 4.

In the Davis Cup Inter-zone final, Vines' games touched bottom. He was routed by a super-steady Austin, 6 – 1, 6 – 1, 6 – 4. The Englishman handled Vines' deliveries much more easily than on the fast turf of Wimbledon.

In his last Davis Cup match against Perry, Vines sprained his ankle in the fourth set. He gallantly continued, only to faint in a heap on court when Perry reached match point. The score in Perry's favour was 1 – 6, 6 – 4, 4 – 6, 7 – 5, 7 – 6 (40 – 15).

In America, Vines lost 6 – 2, 6 – 4, 6 – 4 to Shields at Newport. And to aggravate his depressed frame of mind, a committee was formed, just before the American championships, to question his amateur status. Vines, completely vindicated, declared he was overjoyed. Tension released, Vines reacted. Now only a shadow of his all-conquering self, he was beaten in the fourth round at Forest Hills by Bitsy Grant 6 – 3, 6 – 3, 6 – 3.

In October, 1933, Vines followed Cochet's suit and turned professional. His decision shook the U.S. authorities, for no great player had renounced amateur status so early in his career.

Vines beat Tilden over a series, and never lost to Cochet. In 1934 he played great tennis at Wembley and completely regained his wonderful form in 1935.

After touring Japan and China with Tilden in 1936, Vines defeated Stoeffen on an American tour. In 1937 he drew level with Perry, 37-all. Although forty pounds heavier, and devoting much time to golf, Vines beat Perry 49 – 35 in 1938, and only lost to Donald Budge, 17 – 22, in the following year.

With animosity now forgotten, Vines was officially invited to coach eighteen-year-old Jack Kramer in 1939. His skill helped to produce another world beater.

His achievements at tennis, the game that first brought him fame, will never be forgotten. A shooting star, Vines rocketed across the amateur sky of 1932, blazing a spectacular trail of controlled speed and cannon-ball services.

7: Fred Perry

Once in every decade or so, sport produces a performer who, ignoring existing techniques, follows a new approach which leads to the top of the tree at his or her period of history.

The body rotational style of javelin throwing, the diving method of high jumping and the cradle shot technique of billiards come quickly to mind while in tennis Hadow's use of the lob, Myer's introduction of the overarm service, S. W. Gore's volleying, Dwight Davis' development of the American twist service and McLoughlin's comet-like utilisation of the cannon-ball service all left permanent time markers in the histories of their respective sports; there are, of course, many more cases which could be cited.

In the cases of the tennis examples, however, it must be realised that all arose in the early days when the game was developing.

By the late 1920s and early 1930s all modern techniques had been developed. Men like John Doeg and Frank Shields were following every serve, first and second, to the net, so continuing the method used by Jean Borotra in twice winning Wimbledon.

No one in history has had his service measured to reveal a greater end-to-end of court speed than Ellsworth Vines. There can never have been a better exploiter of 'dinking' as a defence against net attacks than George Lott. Others had enjoyed their moments of triumph through ferocious driving, ceaseless retrieving and, unbelievably almost in men's doubles, through continuous lobbing. It seemed all was known about techniques.

Then early in 1928 a lithe, fast moving, extremely fit young Londoner began to enjoy success with a new groundstroke approach that, during its early development period, had led to members of his club asking him to abandon the style because he was spoiling their social tennis by driving too many balls full pitch into the back stop; the bottom of the net was, it seemed, his other primary target.

The 'revolutionary' was Fred Perry, born 18th May, 1909, the son of a Labour M.P., former pupil at Ealing County School and already world table tennis champion when he became serious about tennis.

His tennis beginnings followed the pattern of so many other world stars. He first borrowed his father's racket and then acquired a new one from the C.W.S. He picked up his early knowledge of the game and its techniques at the Brentham Garden Suburb Club. With eager and ambitious school friends, he kept goal while they practised their soccer shooting or bowled for them to improve their cricket batting, all the time patiently waiting till it was their turn to feed him with returns on the nearby tennis courts.

True to pattern of the days, he spent his school holidays competing in junior tournaments. The Middlesex County at the Herga Club, Harrow, the schoolboys' championships at Queen's Club, Kensington, and even the Junior Championships of Great Britain at the incomparable All-England Lawn Tennis and Croquet Club, Wimbledon.

He performed moderately but there were others of his age group who outshone him. Boys like Bob Tinkler, now a nylon scientist, Ted Avory, currently a V.I.P. in the Lawn Tennis Association and International tennis administration, and the tremendously talented John Olliff who died in 1951.

Though he reached the doubles final in the Middlesex at Herga there was little to suggest he would later dominate Wimbledon and the world scene during the years 1934, 1935 and 1936 or that his would be the decisive role in Britain's Davis Cup winning campaign of 1934 and its retention in 1935, 1936 and 1937.

Yet the Herga campaign was to prove decisive for there, almost uniquely in the 1920s, they really cared about juniors and so Perry joined the club, pairing with Frank Wilde, now a coach at Wimbledon but then the most exciting prospect in Britain, if not Europe.

At that stage Perry's main asset was his speed of foot, a result, many believed, of exceptional eyesight and speed of reaction. His hitting was relatively soft, however, and Britain can be thankful that one of the driving forces then behind English tennis in general, and Middlesex juniors in particular, was the late A. R. 'Pops' Summers, a mainspring of the tournament world as a Slazenger company executive.

'Pops', taken by Perry's enthusiasm and athleticism, saw quickly that his game lacked speed and force. Realising that Perry should be capable of taking every return soon after each bounce, he suggested a winter spent developing this 'early ball' technique.

Like many continental players, Perry gripped his racket somewhat similarly to the average man using a hammer but with the side of the hammer in the plane of the racket strings.

This grip – it is known as the 'continental' – enables groundstrokes, volleys, service, everything to be made without any change of grip. However, this advantage is normally offset by a lack of power; few men possess sufficient strength of wrist to generate power without having the palm of the hand behind the racket handle to aid stability and thrust.

The continental, too, adds inches of effective reach on the forehand side and is normally accompanied by a hitting 'groove' slightly nearer to the ground than the 'grooves' which evolve naturally from the more orthodox grips, in which the hand feels to be behind the racket rather than on top of it.

So the continental grip is well suited to 'scramblers' whose basic idea is simply to reach and return everything hit by the opponent until he finally errs in desperation.

Its application as a basically aggressive grip had scarcely been realised and it is doubtful if even the highly knowledgeable 'Pops' Summers could have realised the use to which Perry would put this grip, remembering that this was in the 1920s.

Nevertheless, 'Pops' said take every ball early and do not worry too much where it goes.

Perry followed his advice faithfully – so faithfully that fellow members of the Herga Club complained bitterly that their Saturday afternoon and Sunday games were being ruined and that too many balls were being lost. The pressure was great but Perry resisted and persisted to the point of losing his place in the club team.

The club controversy spread to the Perry home where his father – the Labour M.P. for Kettering and a moderate player himself – characteristically responded by backing his son to the hilt, culminating in his decision in 1930 to bear the cost and responsibility of taking him out of business and giving him a year of concentrated match and tournament play and intensive practice; but that is running ahead.

Perry's efforts to return each ball soon after its bounce were intended to give him three specific advantages:

(1)   He would save himself time in reaching a volleying position near the net; he was a great and agile volleyer.

(2)   Each extra foot forward cut down the distance the ball travelled by two feet (one foot to him, one foot going away) so that the opponent was hustled more.

(3)   The ball itself was travelling faster when he hit it, so giving a stronger 'rebound' power.

Perry added one major asset of his own – an asset which was to convert the safety-first approach of continental grip technique to the most aggressive game of his era.

Developed from his great physical strength and superb sense of timing, it was a wrist snap or flick not unlike the action of a child whipping a spinning top. It sounds simple enough in theory but is so difficult in actuality that even in the 33 post-Perry amateur days up to 1970 less than a handful of men achieved equal mastery of this technique.

The effect of the wrist snap is to increase racket head velocity and so impart extra power. Those old enough to have seen Perry's championship winning exploits of the 1930s will recall the immense number of winning drives he always produced and the streaming hot faces of the many opponents he hurried into errors and technical breakdown during those halcyon years.

Tennis does not permit measurable comparisons between generations, but, subjectively, it is doubtful if any player before or since has ever hustled his opponents so remorselessly.

So far as Perry's record is concerned, from 1928 through to his signing as a professional in 1937, its progress kept in step with and was governed by his ever-growing mastery of this difficult but effective technique. Almost unplayable at his best, Perry suffered bad days – usually when the atmosphere or opponent or both were second class – and in 1937 he was still wondering if he would ever completely master continental grip stroke play.

Yet stroke play is only one-third of the battle. The other two-thirds come from the character, and that his lacked nothing was amply proved when he sacrificed the immediacy of his position in the 1927-28 Herga match team for the long-term object of greater fame by persevering with an inherently dangerous technique.

Ambition, of course, supplied the driving force. He had first seen tennis by peering over the fence of Devonshire Park, Eastbourne, where the once very important South of England Championships were staged. He also noticed the long lines of cars surrounding the ground. Asking his father who owned them, the then 14-year-old boy was told 'The tennis players'. Deciding that if tennis players all owned cars, that was the game for him, Perry began playing immediately and enjoyed it so much that he and one or two school friends were not above playing truant to sneak down to the local club for a little practice at football, tennis and cricket in turn. One other of the group, Dudley Pope, was also to find some fame later as a county cricketer.

Ambition, flair, industry and a technique completely new in the late 1920s began to make themselves felt in 1929 when Perry struggled through the qualifying competition at Roehampton and so made his first Wimbledon appearance. Qualifiers normally go out in the first or second rounds. Characteristically, Perry won through two rounds before meeting his bête noire,

Olliff. As he was sometimes to repeat when Perry was nearing the height of his fame, Olliff won.

Nevertheless, the fire was fed rather than damped. The mere thrill of competing in the world's premier event boosted Perry's confidence enormously. In August 1928 he had lost somewhat easily to the steady Bill Powell in the quarter-finals at New Malden. Oozing with post Wimbledon confidence, he reached the 1929 final and on a sunny afternoon worthy of the occasion he gave a foretaste of what later followed by hustling Wilfred Freeman into a 6 – 3, 6 – 1 defeat. The court was red but no redder than the panting, sporting man he beat. He, of all present, realised that Perry's first-ever win of an unrestricted tournament would soon be followed by many more.

The decision to remove Perry from work came in time for him first to compete as a 'free man' at Bournemouth in the 1930 Hard Court Championships of Great Britain. It was a dramatic start, for he met the richly talented H. W. 'Bunny' Austin who was being hailed universally as a coming Wimbledon champion. In fact he reached the final twice, was twice ranked second in the world's top ten and in Britain's glorious Davis Cup years of 1933, 1934, 1935 and 1936 equalled Perry in the glittering array of victims who fell to his skills.

So when the still relatively unknown Perry lost only after holding match point it should have been apparent that Britain at last had a potentially outstanding pair of players on whom to base great hopes for the future.

Strangely, this did not happen. Perry's 'early ball' techniques had yet to impress themselves upon all but a handful of experts. At Wimbledon two months later realisation began to dawn. Perry reached the last 16, there falling to the current British number one Dr Colin Gregory, but only after eliminating the seeded Baron H. L. de Morpurgo, the formidable, hard-hitting Italian number one. Played at hurricane speed on an outside court, it ended with Morpurgo hot, flustered and beaten three sets to one.

Suddenly realisation dawned. Britain's Lawn Tennis Association appreciated his potential. Perry was selected for his first tour, a long one that took in the U.S.A., Brazil, the Argentine, Chile and Uruguay.

Beginning in the U.S.A., Perry won his first overseas cup – as doubles runner-up at Westchester with Harold Lee as his partner. A slightly older campaigner than Perry and a kindly man, Lee readily agreed that Perry should have the cup to send home to his father.

As at Wimbledon, Perry reached the last 16 in the American National Championships, losing to John Van Ryn. One of the all-time greats in doubles, van Ryn's forceful, imaginative methods remained a source of trouble right until the end of Perry's amateur career.

At Forest Hills Britain's touring team played a match against the U.S.A., Perry meeting Ellsworth Vines for the first time and losing to him in the final set. History shows that Vines thwarted Perry's ambitions more than any other player, but from that day they struck up a friendship that exists still and which was to make them partners in business seven years later.

Gaining in experience and confidence, Perry improved rapidly and at Buenos Aires won the first major title of the tour, the Argentinian singles championship.

The spring of 1931 provided another thrill for Perry, if not for the British tennis public. Harold Lee, Colin Gregory and Ian Collins all decided it was time to concentrate on their businesses or professions and so let it be known they would not be available for Davis Cup play. After unimpressive trials at Queen's Club, Perry, Austin, Charles Kingsley and Patrick Hughes were chosen with the late H. Roper Barrett as their non-playing captain.

In 1931 Davis Cup selection was the height of most players ambitions, so that even a lukewarm press failed to dampen Perry's spirits. Not that there was any special reason to anticipate the success which followed.

The campaign began at Plymouth against a weak team from Monaco who were further depressed by the transition from Mediterranean sunshine to Devonian dampness. Britain dropped only 21 games in the 15 sets which made up the tie, Perry

beating R. Gallope 6 – 0, 6 – 1, 6 – 2; with the tie won, C. H.
Kingsley played the alternative single.

This runaway win was followed by the French Championships, where Perry failed to fathom the problems of playing a
man with two forehand drives, no matter where the ball was
sent, namely Georgio de Stefani, the ambidextrous Italian. He,
incidentally, became a noted administrator and was President
of the International Lawn Tennis Federation 37 years later when
'open' tennis finally became a fact.

Britain next met a strong South African team at Eastbourne,
where, to the surprise of many, they won 5 – 0.

One week later Japan suffered the same fate and Britain were
in the final of the European zone. No less significant, both Perry
and Bunny Austin beat the late Jiro Satoh, who was regarded
as a top-class world star and who ended the year ninth in the
world.

Public pessimism yielded to optimism – and was quickly
squashed at Wimbledon where Perry reached the semi-finals.
Austin fared slightly worse, reaching match point against Frank
Shields. Then he lost, so accentuating general disappointment
that followed Perry's defeat by Sidney Wood; a win would have
given him the singles as Shields injured himself and Wood was
crowned champion without playing the final.

From Wimbledon the team made a Sunday dash – well,
almost dash, there was scarcely any air travel then – to Prague
where the Czechs, headed by the giant Roderic Menzel, waited
in eager anticipation of a win that turned out to be a 4 – 1
defeat.

Britain were in the inter-zone final but now, surely, the end
had come. Shields and Wood were their singles players, and
look what had happened at Wimbledon. Austin began the tie
well by beating Wood but Perry lost to Shields and he and
Hughes went down in doubles.

All seemed over but Perry showed then what he was to repeat
so often in the next six years – that he would never lightly let
himself down. It may not have been the finest tennis of his
career but Wood could not break it down. So Perry avenged

Wimbledon, Austin followed by simply outclassing Shields and the Challenge Round, a feat beyond British capabilities since 1919, had been reached.

The unexpectedness of this was emphasised when the news leaked out that the Americans had booked hotel and return travel for after the Challenge Round, so sure were they of winning.

France, still at the peak of her tennis glory, proved too strong – just. Perry began his Challenge Round career by beating Jean Borotra 6 – 4 in the fifth set, a Homeric performance before French partisanship at the Stade Roland Garros, but was not yet quite the equal of Henri Cochet. With the match tied two rubbers all, Cochet rose to the occasion, calling out all his genius and experience to beat Perry 6 – 4, 1 – 6, 9 – 7, 6 – 3.

Folowing a celebration dinner given by Britain's L.T.A. at the Savoy Hotel, a British team of Perry and George Patrick Hughes sailed for America.

At Newport Perry beat Keith Gledbill, Wilmer Allison and Sidney Wood but in the final lost to Vines. Thrice more on the tour Vines beat Perry, including the National Championships semi-final after Perry had won the first two sets.

So Cochet and Vines were still his superior but Perry was learning fast. He ended the year ranked fourth in the world, an immense jump from 1930 when he was merely a promising newcomer to the international scene. As so often happens, reaction set in and 1932, the year of hope, became one of bitter disappointment.

At Wimbledon he lost to Crawford in the quarter-final round and Britain reached the third round of the Davis Cup in which they met Germany in Berlin. With the score two-all, Perry lost the first two sets to Dr Daniel Prenn, recovered to reach match point in the fifth set and was beaten by a volley which just pitched on. Prenn went on to win 6 – 2, 6 – 4, 3 – 6, 0 – 6, 7 – 5 and Germany, maddeningly, advanced to the zone final. Three years later Prenn moved to England where, in 1969, as head of a giant communications corporation, he is one of the country's leading industrialists and quite a generous patron of British tennis.

One omen lightened the year, Perry's win in the Pacific South-West Singles Championship at Los Angeles. In the five previous years the Los Angeles winner became American National champion the next year. The pattern held up for Perry, who beat J. Satoh in the final to maintain the tradition, but at the end of 1932 his world ranking sank to seventh.

During this time Perry was steadily developing his attacking play and gaining confidence but there still remained a suspicion, based on a few uncomfortable defeats, that his backhand was vulnerable to volleying attacks from the net.

Norman Farquharson, a South African Cambridge blue – intensified them at Wimbledon, where, in the second round, he brilliantly volleyed Perry to humiliation. But the Davis Cup atoned for this, Britain crushing the apparently invincible Americans 4 – 1 and then beating France 3 – 2 in a Challenge Round which few who saw or heard it over the radio are ever likely to forget.

Borotra had retired – temporarily – from singles; he continued to announce his retirement annually until 1969, when he was still going strong in veterans doubles at the age of 70. Rene Lacoste had been laid low by illness and André Merlin, a brilliant 19-year-old youngster, was brought in.

Perry began the tie well by beating Cochet but for the first and only time in his life fainted on his way back to the dressing-room. This became a big bogy in British minds and there was considerable consternation when the rubber score reached two-all and Perry had to play Merlin in the fifth, deciding, rubber.

The situation looked grim. Perry was still so ragged that he had been rested from the doubles and banished from the practice court after only five minutes on the previous day.

Underdog Merlin had all to gain and nothing to lose and there were 12,000 yelling Frenchmen spurring him on from the stands.

Maybe in normal conditions Perry could have used his superb

attacking methods to crush Merlin but that day they were not on.

Merlin attacked like a fury, took the first set and reached set point in the second. Using his superb physical attributes, Perry chased and clung, staying tight with the Frenchman and believing the crack would come. It did, Merlin missing an easy smash on the set point. Though his chance had gone, Merlin showed no signs of realisation and it took all Perry's remarkable powers of concentration and fight to battle Britain to the Davis Cup Championship 4 – 6, 8 – 6, 6 – 2, 7 – 5.

Perry did not see the actual presentation. He was flat out and exhausted in the dressing-room. But also tremendously satisfied, both as a patriot and as an individual who had survived just about the ultimate test of his skill and nerve.

Clearly, there was nothing now except his own powers of applied concentration to prevent a long domination of the world tennis scene. There remained, perhaps, the need to prove to himself that he could 'fence' with his backhand since, technically, his early ball system made it impossible for him ever to develop a traditional, long-swing drive of the type exemplified by, say, Donald Budge in 1937 and 1938.

Experience in tennis is a good teacher and Perry learnt his lessons, supplying conclusive proof when he beat Jack Crawford 6 – 3, 6 – 0, 7 – 5 in July 1934 to become the first British winner of the Wimbledon singles since S. W. Gore in 1909.

In the 1933 American final Perry attacked Crawford into defeat. On the billiard-table smooth Wimbledon centre court Perry decided a repeat of those tactics would give Crawford too many definite targets. He decided to slow Crawford down a little by running him around the court for a set. Then, having taken away his edge, to move over to more positive and obvious methods of attack.

To rely on such a strategy spoke volumes for Perry's growing confidence in that backhand and just one set was amply sufficient to justify that confidence, for the backhand responded fully to every demand made on it.

In previous rounds Perry had faltered near to defeat, notably against Wood in the semi-final where he won only by 6 – 3 in the fifth set.

Crawford led 5 – 4 and forty – love in the third set of the final and if . . . But there was no 'if'. Probably because of the pressure Perry applied, he made mistakes and no extra sets were needed.

From then until he turned professional in 1937, Perry bestrode international tennis as few men have done before or since. Naturally fit, he did nothing to jeopardise that fitness. The apparent gin and tonic was merely a tonic and the pipe between his teeth normally proved, on examination, to be empty, never alight; or so testify friends who have known him over 40 years. Sensible eating has left him, in 1969, with measurements identical to 1936, so that he remains the immaculate 'clothes horse' he was early in 1936 when, in return for endorsement, Simpsons of Piccadilly offered him a sixpenny royalty on every pair of Daks trousers they ever sold, a deal that would have earned him several million pounds sterling. But the amateur rules of those days prohibited amateurs from such contracts and he was not yet ready to turn professional. Apart from all else, Perry wished for Britain to hold the Davis Cup for one more year. Such is the commercialism of modern, open tennis, such concern for one's country is now difficult to comprehend. Yet given his youth back and put into present-day international tennis, Perry's attitude forces belief that he would again put country before self.

Yet, strangely, he so preferred the American way of life that he became a naturalised citizen of the U.S.A. in 1937.

It is impossible to measure the influence Perry exerted on British tennis. His efforts, backed by those of Austin, raised its status to the level it enjoyed in the days of the Doherty brothers 30 years earlier. Yet his individual style was not one to be imitated lightly and, strangely, it is doubtful if he ever fully appreciated this himself, so that his influence later as a teacher and guide never approached the contribution he made to British tennis as a player.

In any assessment of the game's 'best-evers' Perry must rank high – certainly within the top half-dozen. Equally certainly, he would have had no trouble at all in adapting to modern serve-volley methods. Indeed, such was his speed of eye and reflex, he would surely have developed more than adequate antidotes.

He brought to tennis a new technique. In considering his career one wonders what other techniques he could or would have conceived in the era of Rod Laver, John Newcombe and Arthur Ashe.

8: Donald Budge

Shortly before noon on 10th November, 1938 many of America's leading tennis writers exchanged knowing glances across the New York law chambers of Walter Pate, non-playing captain of the Davis Cup Champion nation, America.

Though they had not been told any official reason for the summons to attend, all knew they were about to hear that Pate's greatest team asset and tennis playing friend, Donald Budge, was forsaking amateurism for the then less prestigious but more lucrative field of professional tennis.

Twelve months earlier many of those present had chided Budge for turning his back on a $50,000 contract.

That action and the actual reception room in which they waited offered two glaring clues to Budge's uniqueness.

To understand why, it is necessary to forget the ambience of still relatively new Open tennis and recall the 1930s. Then, despite reasonably abundant shamateurism, top tennis was predominantly amateur in attitudes and control. It was also highly regarded socially. Three great American players, Bill Tilden, Ellsworth Vines and Vincent Richards had previously signed professional contracts – and had suffered virtual ostracism by the United States Lawn Tennis Association.

Yet here was Budge, a bare two months away from his world record-breaking feat of winning the Australian, French, Wimbledon and American championships in one year and hero of America's successful retention of the Davis Cup, receiving unprecedented official blessing for his desertion to the ranks of the then highly suspect play-for-pay circus!

Journalistic surprise yielded to sheer disbelief when those reporters were ushered into the room where drama was about to unfold, for there at Pate's desk stood Holcombe Ward, President of the United States Lawn Tennis Association.

Historically one of the world's greatest tennis administrators, Ward graced his position with all the integrity and love of the game first shown by him as an American champion and Davis Cup player in the 1890s and 1900s. He had long been regarded as the primary guardian of amateur tennis, yet here he was launching America's – probably the world's – greatest-ever tennis player into a field which meant almost certain loss of the Davis Cup and, inevitably, a substantial reduction in amateur gate receipts during the coming year.

True, there was ample reason for gratitude that Budge had delayed this irrevocable step for twelve key months. But this blessing, this show of deep affection for the modest, freckle-faced, 6 feet 3 inch redhead between Ward and Pate, this was the lion and the lamb lying down together with a vengeance.

Understanding can be gained only through a close study of the modest, polite, level-headed youngster – Budge was still only 23 years old – whose own integrity, loyalty and love of tennis had swept aside all defences and resentments in the then most conservative governing body in the entire tennis world.

Budge's character had shone like an inspiring beacon since his first tournament venture when aged 15, but it reached dazzling brilliance when, in the autumn of 1937, he turned his back upon a fortune that would have given him security for life.

He had ended ten years of American Davis Cup humiliation, brought home all three Wimbledon titles and added the American crown to it.

He became the first tennis player ever to head the poll among America's top 600 sportswriters for the outstanding amateur athlete of the year, so capturing the coveted Sullivan Trophy.

The temptations to accept the $50,000 contract were immense, the pressures of his closest friends almost unendurable.

He knew the chance to give his ageing father and mother a few extra comforts might never rise again.

Yet overriding all this loomed his omnipresent sense of

obligation to a game which had bestowed on him such un-
believable honours and to the generous, selfless administrators
who had helped make it all possible.

There was no flag waving or tub thumping. Indeed, no
thoughts of heroics or martyrdom ever crossed his mind. He
believed he owed tennis a debt and this he humbly set out to
repay.

Little wonder the U.S. L.T.A. thought him the salt of the
earth, and little wonder that a man of such immense character
should have risen from tennis obscurity to world pre-eminence
in the short spell of seven years.

How strange, then, that until he reached the age of 15 he
didn't like tennis – even thought it 'cissy', an understand-
able attitude in the soccer-mad son of a former Glasgow
Ranger.

Not that his father encouraged the hours his beanpole younger
son spent waiting in the streets to start impromptu 'kick arounds'
with other willing kids. Injury had once all but cost Don's
father his life and so anxiety that the gangling Donald might
suffer similarly is easy to understand.

Don's older brother, Lloyd, had long since caught the fever
of tennis madness. No price would have been too high for him
if tennis greatness could have been bought. But eminence
demands skills and personality traits lacking in Lloyd, though he
later gained sweet solace in becoming one of the world's greatest
coaches.

Part of Lloyd's teaching skill lay in recognising latent
potential and there it abounded in his younger brother.

Encouraged by his father, mother and sister Jean, Lloyd used
every known form of persuasion to tempt Donald on to the
nearby courts in Oakland, California.

He met with scant response and from eleven through to fifteen
Donald never touched a racket. Basketball – he was a fine player
– baseball, roller-skating, marbles and, above all, football carried
far greater appeal. When not at play Donald busied himself in
his father's toolshed, showing quite a quota of craftsmanship
in the things he produced for Jean and himself.

So life continued busily and contentedly for the Budges until a fateful supper back in June 1930.

'There's a tournament on next week,' chided Lloyd, 'why don't you start playing again and see if you can beat some of the other boys?'

Amid much happy leg-pulling Donald remained silent. Next morning he dived in the cupboard, unearthed a racket and set off for the courts for a spell of sustained practice. Each day that week he repeated the routine and on the following Monday he began his unlikely quest for the Californian State Boys' Championship. Unheralded and unsung, playing in corduroy pants, he zoomed through to the final. There, in hastily acquired whites, he downed Paul Newton 6 – 0, 6 – 4 to win the first tournament in which he ever competed.

Ambition fired by this unexpected 15th birthday present, he decided immediately to stay with tennis and set himself the first of many step by step stages which eventually culminated in his 1938 'Grand Slam' of the four major international championships.

There was plenty of blood, sweat and tears along the way. His second ambition was the Californian Junior (18 and under) title, but he lost twice in the final to Charles Hunt before gaining revenge and the Championship in 1933.

He did even better that year, for, competing now in senior as well as junior events, he beat Edward Chandler and Bobby Riggs in becoming the first man to win the California Junior and Senior Championships in the same year.

By now first whispers of 'He's going to be great' were reaching the ears of Northern California L.T.A. Officials. Though red-headed, he then had none of the dynamic fiery power of his Californian predecessor Maurice McLoughlin, inventor and first exploiter of the now commonplace cannon-ball service.

Instead, Donald relied on backcourt stability and a mobility rare in so tall a man for wearing down and breaking the more venturesome opposition with whom he clashed.

But those in the know search below the surface and it did

not take them long to see in Donald a near-perfect sense of timing and balance.

Later, he became feared for sheer all-round power. Probably no man in tennis has come near the average groundspeed miles per hour he imparted to the ball with every stroke he produced. Yet all who watched his golden years at Wimbledon vow they never saw him make an ugly stroke or mistime the ball, no matter how severely harried or hurried he might have been.

So, potential discovered, he was sent across America to the National Junior Championships towards the end of 1933. Official confidence was justified for he won the title, beating in the final Gene Mako with whom he struck up a partnership and friendship that later brought most of the game's highest honours.

Budge's strength then lay in his backhand, a stroke which stayed in an unvarying groove throughout his entire career. Though a right-hander, schoolboy Donald was a 'southpaw' when batting at baseball. Beginning tennis with Lloyd's 15-ounce racket, he needed both hands when returning shots hit to his backhand. This and the baseball, he always insisted, developed the unique, beautifully flowing stroke which many experts rate as the finest ever seen.

As with so many champions before and since, Donald met and finally conquered continuous problems with the forehand. A Californian, he was raised on cement courts where the normal bounce is high; the average hitting level is around the shoulder compared with waist or even knee height on turf.

Historically, this has resulted in the development of a style of forehand drive peculiar to California and Johannesburg, South Africa, where conditions are similar. In this style, the palm of the hand is below the handle. It is called the 'Western' grip forehand.

Though effective in the relatively few areas where the ball bounces high, it is dangerously vulnerable on grass courts where the ball skids through on a low trajectory, and the world's main events take place on grass.

Lloyd, Donald's coach, was well aware of such considerations and so taught his talented brother the 'Eastern' grip drive which, because the palm is behind the handle, is far better suited to grass.

Unfortunately, this stroke is far less spectacular than the 'Western' and, coincidentally, at that moment in time America's top men stars all used obsolescent 'Western' forehands. Understandably but unwisely, Donald forsook the stroke he had been taught and for four frustrating years suffered enormous problems in first realising his mistake and then rectifying it. In returning to an 'Eastern' orthodox stroke Donald was helped immeasurably by Sydney Wood and Fred Perry, both great Wimbledon champions, and the coach at the local Claremont Club, Tom Stow.

Donald's 1933 trip East began and ended at Culver, Indiana, but in 1934 his state association wisely decided he was ripe for the glittering circuit of Eastern grass courts tournaments culminating in the American National Championships at Forest Hills.

His début took place in New Jersey at the Seabright Lawn Tennis and Cricket Club, one of the most famous and respected in the entire country. Its record of previous winners read like a tennis 'Who's Who'.

It took Donald one – just one – match to realise the stupidity of his changed forehand drive. Playing against a man whose sliced drives kept the ball low, he was in continual trouble. Surviving, he awoke on the second day to find rain had dampened the grass and that the ball was sliding through even lower than on the previous day.

His conqueror was Henry Prusoff of Seattle, who, though he never won a place among America's top ten men, was a useful and experienced tournament competitor.

One week later at Longwood, Berkeley Bell, then his country's number seven, allowed the saddened Donald only three games.

Ironically, both Prusoff and Bell used 'Western' forehands, Bell to produce a wicked chop shot which sizzled the ball through repeatedly at ankle height.

Though depressed and to some degree outplayed by these two men, Donald remained clear headed. Their success with a shot he, too, favoured did not blind him to its inherent short-comings.

A victory over tenth-ranking American Bitsy Grant in the National Championships yielded some consolation and stoked the fires of ambition once again.

Returning home, Donald immediately began a long corres-pondence with Wood whose detailed letters helped incalculably in Donald's return to orthodoxy on the forehand. Particularly, Wood stressed the importance of self-confidence and it is difficult to decide whether his advocacy or Donald's keenness was the more effective factor in the eventual evolvement of this then weak wing into an offensive weapon equalling the backhand.

Not that Donald went the full limit of change during that first winter of discontent and frequent discouragement. He changed his grip only to half way between the 'Western' and 'Eastern' and did not complete the modification until 1937 after closely studying the way in which Fred Perry's footwork enabled him to take the ball when running at full speed, particularly in a forward direction. Not content merely with watching, Donald sought personal advice from Perry, who was generosity itself in the assistance he gave.

Donald's dedication and seriousness matched his natural talents, a fact not lost upon the U.S. L.T.A. who showed their faith by sending him overseas for the first time.

Their decision was in some measure simplified because Ells-worth Vines and Lester Stoeffen were now professionals, Wilmer Allison headed the rankings and Sidney Wood and Frank Shields, ranked two and three respectively, asked not to be chosen for the European trip.

Clearly, America needed a younger team if a decade of Davis Cup humiliation was to be succeeded by long-wished-for triumph.

So Donald, along with Gene Mako, was chosen; the youngster who had not competed in a senior tournament until he was 18 years old, was to play at Wimbledon soon after his 20th birthday.

Donald began his first overseas trip by beating C. M. Jones – now the editor of the British L.T.A.'s official journal *Lawn*

Tennis but then edging up for eventual Davis Cup recognition – 6 – 4, 6 – 4 in the London Grass Courts Championships. Both men received generous praise in British newspapers, most of which carried immediate forecasts of the great heights Donald would eventually scale. Yet not one of the perceptive correspondents who wrote the stories fully realised the true potential of the lean, 6 foot 3 inch red-headed giant with the freckled face, amiable grin, and powerful style. For when the crunch comes – and it comes all too often in the tense conditions of championship tennis – it is character and self-reliance that govern the then margin separating true greatness from the levels just below it.

Though losing both his singles – to Fred Perry and Bunny Austin – in the Davis Cup Challenge Round, Donald justified the faith shown in him with a string of fine wins, headed by one over Austin at Wimbledon and others from Gottfried von Cramm and Henner Henkel in the Davis Cup interzone final.

Returning from Europe, he soon suffered a humiliating defeat by a tiny, mobile 'brick-wall' from Atlanta, Bryan M. (Bitsy) Grant. From this he finally realised that without a powerful net game he would always be vulnerable to clever, defensive retrieving men of similar resource to Grant.

He resolved to remedy this deficiency but an encore by Grant early in 1936 confirmed Donald's need of a merciless net game. He redoubled his efforts, both in practice and under the stress of competitive conditions.

This second defeat by Grant – it was at White Sulphur Springs – provided a large gallery with a now historic instance of Donald's supreme good behaviour and sunny disposition.

After leading two sets to love Donald was teased and tormented by the way in which 'Bitsy', the 'Atlanta Atom', scrambled back seeming winners with heartbreaking regularity and monotony. From the verge of victory Donald tailed away to the edge of defeat.

A long rally began and Donald, desperate, moved to the net behind a deep drive. Grant, ever resourceful, threw up a splendid lob which, somehow, Donald got under to thunder a blinding

Ellsworth Vines

Fred Perry

Donald Budge

Jack Kramer

smash far beyond even this five-feet two-inch packet of perpetual motion.

Stung beyond endurance by the perfection of the shot and the crisis of the moment, Bitsy screamed furiously, 'You redhead'.

For a moment it seemed Donald would explode too. Then a wide grin spread slowly across his homely face and from his six feet three inches he looked down on tiny Bitsy. 'I'll see you outside after the match, Bitsy,' he called across the net, so converting an electric situation into one of warm good humour.

This instinct for easing a crisis was proved even more dramatically in the Davis Cup interzone final against Germany at Wimbledon in July 1937. Now halfway through a year that was to establish his world supremacy, Donald was locked in the fifth and deciding rubber with von Cramm. Already Wimbledon champion, there had seemed little reason to believe the magnificently talented and sporting German could cause undue difficulty to Donald.

But Cramm, though he never won Wimbledon, ranks high among the all-time greats; it was his misfortune to mature in the era dominated by such giants as Fred Perry and then Don Budge.

On this day Cramm, possibly subconsciously realising how his antagonism towards the Nazis was endangering his personal safety, plumbed far below the normal depths of effort to register a new standard of greatness for his beloved Fatherland.

Donald, in top form, could do little. Down two sets to love, he somehow raised his game beyond excellence to square the sets, only for Cramm to climb higher still to reach 4 – 1 in the fifth set.

From non-playing captain Walter Pate downwards, every American national and supporter faced inevitable defeat. Pate, in mental agony, strove to hide his suffering but his face told all.

Pausing by Pate's chair at the change of ends, Donald reassured his captain 'Don't worry, Cap. I won't let you down. I'll win this one if it kills me.'

Then he strode down to begin a recovery that still chokes the voices of witnesses when recalling the events that happened.

C

Determined to complete a German triumph and urged on by the cheers of a crowd knowledgeable about his sportsmanship and ideals, the blond aristocrat lifted his game yet another impossible notch.

Donald lifted his too. No statistics are – were – available for who viewing such tennis could do aught else but watch and wonder.

If there were enforced errors from then until the end they could have been counted on the fingers of one hand.

If tennis balls could talk those used would surely have claimed they suffered the hardest hammering in history.

Spellbound, the earlier partisan crowd applauded each point with near hysterical fervour. Superb shots gushed until they were commonplace. Excellence dazzled and near the end only miracles appeared sufficient to win the ceaseless succession of breathtaking rallies.

Gradually Donald clawed his way level and into a lead. Stubbornly, inflexibly he forced his way inexorably to 7 – 6, advantage United States.

Positioning himself with his customary bottomwaggle – copied from Vines – Donald thundered over a seeming ace. Adrenalin flowing freely, Cramm pounced, rifling back a flashing drive which also looked a winner. So a short rally developed with Cramm rushing netwards behind a fierce drive deep in the corner of Donald's forehand court.

Streaking along the baseline, booming the ball without pause in his run, Donald climaxed this never-to-be-forgotten epic with one of the greatest shots in history, a thundering forehand low over the net and flying as if guided by the entire length of the sideline.

The ball pitched inches from the baseline, Donald's promise to Pate was kept and the faultless German held out a generous hand of congratulation, a smile cloaking the agony of near certainty of disaster to follow; prison based on the most dubious of allegations.

Even in this moment of supreme glory Donald remained sensitive to others for, as he later told Pate, he thought as they shook hands 'Gottfried, you certainly have got more out of tennis than any player who has won everything.'

Two months later, in the American singles championship final, Cramm again forced Donald to a fifth set . . . and again sparked off a holocaust of firepower. Maintaining a 90 miles per hour volley, ground stroke pace and serving around 110 m.p.h., Donald raced through the set 6 – 1 while conceding only four errors; all thunderous drives, the most inaccurate of them only missing its target by four or five inches.

There were still triumphs to come, obstacles to overcome, decisions to make. Growing up, too, had its place, though by now the once shy young boy with the homespun air was confident enough to copy his great friend Mako in taking his place at the drums in Tommy Dorsey's band atop New York's most fashionable hotel.

But his record alone tells the story of his greatness. From July 1937 to September 1938 and subsequent professionalism the honours boards of the world's four major championships record : 1937 Wimbledon; singles, doubles, mixed doubles, 1938 Australian, singles, 1938 French, singles. 1938 Wimbledon, singles, doubles, mixed. 1938 American, singles, doubles, mixed.

There remain two anecdotes which point his character. In protest against the imprisonment of Von Cramm, he refused to re-visit Germany in 1938 although in 1937 he had said he would return.

Later that year, on the eve of his inaugural professional meeting with Ellsworth Vines, it was discovered he had never played on a wood surface court and that he had not been practising at Madison Square Garden.

Urged by friends to do so, his reply was roughly that everyone was extolling his perfections as a tennis player and that if they were right he should not meet with undue difficulty in adjusting his strokes to the pace.

If their assessments were wrong, he would be beaten and this would show that he was indeed fallible.

There was no histrionics about this, merely a quiet determina-

tion to discover for himself just where he really stood in relation-
ship to all the superlatives that were being lavished on him.

For the record, he won comfortably and went on to beat Perry
with similar ease early in the next year.

The intervention of war interrupted his tennis and by its
end a shoulder ailment had imposed a number of technical
deficiencies – measured against his earlier splendours.

Nevertheless, the power of his play remained for over a
decade, forcing Jack Kramer into completely new tennis methods
and theories which left Kramer with the still unchanged opinion
that Budge is the greatest player in the history of tennis. (*Lawn
Tennis*, May 1969 issue.)

In tennis such views are subjective, for there are no stop
watches or measures to fix achievements, but Kramer played
against all stars over an era ranging from Tilden to Hoad and
Rosewall.

What is more certain is that tennis has never produced a
finer sportsman and ambassador and that it remains the richer
for his continued presence as a devoted coach in the U.S.A.

9: Jack Kramer

Professional tennis promoter Jack Harris looked out from a window of New York's Lexington Hotel and winced.

Snow was falling and by early afternoon on Boxing Day, 1947, 15 inches of it was burying the streets to knee height and higher.

'The biggest tennis match in history and nobody will be able to get there to see it,' he bemoaned.

Ten minutes walk away the signs at Madison Square Garden, the traditional American venue for professional débuts, carried words reading 'Pro. tennis tonite. Riggs vs Kramer', but the snow had brought all public transport other than the subway to a halt and private motorists had quit much earlier, leaving their cars littering the streets.

Across the city Weather Bureau experts forecast the storm would continue into the early hours of the next day.

Bobby Riggs, small, slick talking but a master of court strategy, had dethroned Donald Budge as world professional champion at Wembley twelve months earlier. Kramer had swept the amateur world, winning at Wimbledon and Forest Hills with a brand of controlled aggression that was already ranking him high among the all-time greats. Both men expected to win . . . but who would be there to see this 'match of the decade'?

It was too late to postpone the match, so around 7 p.m. the protagonists left the Lexington to make the journey on foot to 'The Garden'. The streets were empty and they almost turned back. When they finally struggled through to their changing rooms their tour supports, Dinny Pails and Pancho Segura, were beginning the preliminary before a near-empty house.

At 9.10, after a record-breaking fall of almost 26 inches, the snow stopped. When Riggs and Kramer emerged around 9.15 they blinked their eyes in utter disbelief. For there, packing the seats, were 15,114 of the 16,052 fans who had bought seats. They had marched in Wellington boots, taken the subways, stomped in snowshoes. Some even arrived on skis. Many had come from their offices without having the chance to return home for their tickets. The box office coped by saying 'Phone home for the seat numbers and we will issue duplicates'.

The total take for the night was a record-breaking $55,730.50 and Riggs won the opener 6 – 2, 10 – 8, 4 – 6, 6 – 4. It was to be one of Riggs' rare wins, for Kramer learnt even faster as a professional than he did as an amateur and on successive tours decimated Riggs (69 to 20 wins), Pancho Gonzales (96 to 27), Pancho Segura and Frank Sedgman.

Financially, the Sedgman tour was his biggest bonanza for he was both player and promoter. As players he and Sedgman each collected a record-breaking $128,000; his take as the promoter has never been revealed. His royalties on the Jack Kramer rackets still being publicised by the Wilson Sporting Goods Company 22 years after he won Wimbledon total over $1 million and it has been assessed that his income exceeds $70,000 a year 'before he gets out of bed'.

All this adds up to a pretty remarkable man. Yet his introduction to the game he has served so well as player, promoter, peace-maker, liaison expert, administrator and T.V./radio commentator scarcely forecast what was to follow.

Born in Las Vegas on 5th August, 1921, his early play days were monopolised by baseball. The change came when his father bought a couple of old rackets and began hitting a ball about for exercise with his then twelve-year-old son.

One year later when the Kramers had moved to San Bernardino the youthful Jack won himself a place in his junior high school team, from which he was sent to play in a tournament in Santa Monica. He was convincingly beaten in the first round and this irritated him enormously because he had always been tops in the various games at school and this had developed in him the outlook of a winner.

His reaction to defeat was typical, for he made up his mind there and then to beat all those children who were around the same size as himself but who at that time were playing much better tennis. Strangely, in that very tournament the major stars were Bobby Riggs and Ted Schroeder, who were to figure so prominently later in his tennis career.

Soon after the Santa Monica debacle he met Californian coach Dick Skeen and for six months took a multitude of lessons. Skeen had a profound effect for he worked very industriously on Kramer's ground strokes and although Kramer became the arch priest of the so-called 'big game' he has consistently advocated the development of sound ground strokes as the basis for any champion.

Beautifully built and a natural athlete Kramer made fairly rapid progress and in 1936 came under the eye of Perry Jones, the giant administrator of Southern Californian tennis and the man responsible for the production of more champions than probably anyone in history.

Jones immediately made him an honorary member of the Los Angeles Tennis Club, where Kramer had daily opportunities of seeing Ellsworth Vines, Donald Budge and all the great Californian stars of those times in action. This was at the time of Vines' heyday and the influence of this other great Californian was always apparent in Kramer's game.

Consistent practice and match play against such strong opposition coupled to the skilled coaching given by Dick Skeen brought about rapid improvement and in 1935, as an unseeded player, Kramer won the National Boys' Singles.

Perry Jones, though a keen analyst of the technical aspects of tennis, always looked for winners and when Kramer captured this title Jones was convinced that here was a great champion in the making. So he extended his patronage of Kramer and sent him to play in all the Californian tournaments and to travel as far away as Canada for more junior tournaments in the summer of 1937. During that winter he arranged twice-weekly practice with Ellsworth Vines and this continued for three months. He also trained with Fred Perry at the Beverley Hills tennis club which Perry and Vines owned jointly at that time.

With this tremendous practice and the direction and guidance of Vines his game leapt forward and in 1938 he played in all major tournaments, ending the year classified number 15 in the official United States lawn tennis ranking.

One year later, in 1939, he was chosen as a member of the American Davis Cup team to defend the Cup in the challenge round against Australia at Philadelphia. He played in the doubles with the late Joe Hunt and they were beaten by Quist and Gommage. Nevertheless, he was then the youngest player, at 17 years 10 months and 30 days, ever to play in the challenge round and he retained that record until 1968 when John Alexander of Sydney represented Australia at 17 years 5 months and 28 days.

Obviously by now, Kramer was destined for a big future. It was round about this time that he first demonstrated, though only to himself, the enormous strength of character and sound reasoning power which made him the one man who brought order and a sense of responsibility in place of irresponsibility and money-grabbing into the professional game.

He had reached the final of a tournament and on the eve was approached by a shady gambling syndicate who offered him $5,000 to lose this final, together with some veiled threats of what would happen to him if he didn't.

Young, not very rich and somewhat frightened, Kramer faced a tremendous problem and this kept him awake most of the night. But he reasoned that if he accepted this bribe he would never be able to look himself in the face again. Furthermore, he would be inevitably and always in the grip of gamblers and gangsters. So with some fears and trepidations he rejected the offer and won the tournament. In fact there was no retribution.

The European war began in 1939 but tennis continued at a fairly high level for a further two years until the entry of America into the war. Kramer played a considerable amount of tennis but his opportunities were limited. With America's entry into the war he joined the United States Coast Guards and was abroad and out of big tennis until 1946.

Wimbledon resumed in 1946 and Kramer came over with an enormous reputation and as favourite for the title. It was not to be his that year for the tactical wizardry of Jaroslav Drobny on Court 1 allied to the most enormous blisters which came up on Kramer's playing hand cost him the match.

Returning to America he won the United States Championships and then made up his mind that if he won Wimbledon and Forest Hills in 1947 as well as winning both his singles in the Davis Cup challenge round he would turn professional.

He won Wimbledon as expected, receiving his prize from the hands of the late King George VI, a meeting which made him far more jittery than any tennis match he ever played.

Again his sense of perfection and his ambition showed up in his actions. Leaving England for America early on the Sunday morning after the Championships ended he flew to Chicago where he paid approximately one hundred dollars for a series of lessons with Bob Harman, a skilled coach whose writings are well known throughout the English-speaking countries of the world.

Practically any coach in the world would have been honoured and happy to have given Kramer free coaching, but Kramer had a definite object in view and he wanted only the best. More than wanting the best, he wished to pay his way so that he was under no obligation.

Accurately as things turned out, Kramer analysed that in the final of the American Championships he would have to play Frank Parker whose forehand, though a formidable stroke, was not the equal of his backhand. Kramer further analysed that his own cross court forehand driving would on that day have to be impeccable and infallible, and he was not altogether happy with this particular weapon in his stroke armoury. He reckoned Harman would develop it for him and sure enough the Chicago coach did. Parker went into an early lead in that final, but Kramer's remorseless hammering of his forehand eventually brought about Parker's downfall and gave Kramer the title.

Then came the Challenge Round and his signature on a professional contract which began with the match against Riggs.

Kramer virtually introduced into amateur tennis the concept of 'playing the percentages', an approach suggested to him by an engineer, Cliff Roche, who played little tennis himself. Ted Schroeder, the 1949 Wimbledon champion and one of Kramer's closest personal friends, also prospered from Roche's theories.

Put broadly, 'playing the percentages' consists of stroking each individual return in the way that yields the maximum chance of winning the point, either immediately or later in the rally, whilst minimising the likelihood of losing the point.

Mercer Beasley, famed American coach of Ellsworth Vines, Frank Parker and other top stars, had first hit on this attitude when introducing 'zoning' into his coaching back in the late 1920s and early 1930s.

Beasley likened a player's half of the court to traffic signals. Returning the ball from behind the baseline offers little hope of hitting an outright winner. So the risks of hitting very hard or on to a line are heavily outweighed by the dangers of erring. It is a 'red' area and so the 'percentage play' is to allow ample clearance of the net and margin within the line while temporising or manoeuvring for a better chance later in the rally.

The area between the base and service line allows for a more aggressive attitude, how aggressive depending on the pace and height of the opponent's return, his position on the court, the state of the score and so on. It is an 'amber' zone from which one proceeds with some caution – but definitely proceeds.

Returns pitching between the net and service line normally offer every chance for out-and-out attack. The angles offered for a placement are wider, the striker is already en route to the net and the opponent will have reduced time to regain position or make his reply. It is a 'green' area from which the point should be won, either by an immediate and forceful placement or through forcing a weak return which can be killed by a volley at the net.

Because of his geometrical skill and calculating mind, Roche took this theory much farther. In particular, he taught Kramer a theory of angles which maximised his chances of maintaining superior court position in every rally, irrespective of the angle of return.

Kramer's service methods were a good example. The idols of his youth, Vines and Budge, were famed and feared for their cannon-balls. Both served many aces – but both sometimes missed. Neither could be guaranteed to pull out an ace whenever one was needed.

In actuality there was not an enormous difference between their first and second services, but tennis at the summit is governed more by intangibles than techniques. The psychological effect on a receiver facing a crisis is normally strong when the server faults. In his mind he no longer fears being aced and so becomes aggressively minded. He moves forward slightly physically and considerably mentally. Far more than it should, the initiative ebbs from the server towards the receiver.

Kramer, inspired by Roche, calculated the percentage play favoured another approach. Approximately as tall and powerful as Vines and Budge, he was equally capable of producing an ace.

Instead, he developed as his point winners sequence routines that first, with his first service, swung the receiver well out of court. Off their returns he played deep and low to the far corner, moved into the net and then cut off the reply with a volley.

Naturally, he was far too shrewd to become stereotyped. Sometimes he would serve fast down the middle line and run in immediately or he would run in behind his swinging service. Occasionally his first drive would 'wrong foot' the receiver. Always he sought to be one or two thoughts ahead of his opponents . . . And normally he succeeded.

His sequence was related to the point. At thirty-love he might try for an ace down the middle line; at forty-thirty or thirty-forty he seldom did. That was the time for a percentage play.

Written down, this in itself sounds stereotyped; but such was the variety of his overall method of attack and the power and consistency of his stroke play, players of the day – the late 1940s through to the middle 1950s – agreed almost unanimously that Kramer's service was the hardest of all to break, harder even than Gonzales, whose power, agility and will to win ranks him high among the all-time greats.

In the first half-dozen matches Riggs, a master tactician who, in Kramer's view, pioneered modern tennis despite his smallness, more or less held Kramer. Then Kramer's computer-like mind strung together the plays which enable him to establish complete supremacy by the end of their tour.

By then Budge, who had suffered shoulder trouble during the war, was declining but he remained a very great player with, perhaps, the most powerful ground strokes in tennis history.

Kramer had already developed his serve and stay back techniques. His meetings with Budge merely confirmed they were right. 'He returned service so surely and powerfully it simply wasn't possible to follow service to the net with any hope of winning.' Kramer wrote in *Lawn Tennis*.

He says always of Riggs and Budge that they were the men who above all, exercised the most profound effect on his whole approach to match tennis.

Kramer prospered as a contract professional, but two factors soon became crystal clear. The first was that the promoter was making substantial profits. The second was that the professionals were badly organised and unreliable in their dealings to the point of sheer irresponsibility. He soon set himself to the task of changing all this.

Forseeing the possibility of big tournaments attracting large crowds and paying out big prizes, he slowly began promoting and signing up players under contract. Frank Sedgman was his first.

That he was able to withstand all the immense pressures of administration and organisation yet still maintain his position as the world's number one player is just another mark of his uniqueness.

His skill and judgment as a promoter can be measured. From 1947 through to 1968 he consistently showed a profit – a big profit – and he only suffered a loss in his efforts to help Open tennis get off to a good start in April 1968. George MacCall, director of the National Tennis League professional group – Rod Laver, Ken Rosewall and Pancho Gonzales were its star attractions – hesitated about sending these men to Bournemouth for the first-ever Open Championship. The prizes were relatively small and so the cost to MacCall, who had given the men huge guarantees, was going to be great.

To halve the costs, in effect, Kramer undertook to promote a professional tournament at Wembley the week after Bournemouth.

The date clashed with the London Hard Courts Championships at Hurlingham and a British Davis Cup tie. Hurlingham, the L.T.A. and the British Press were angry, the crowds were disappointing.

Kramer lost some £6,000 and a fair degree of prestige, a poor and unjust return for a genuine effort to help.

Not that he or his friends would claim he never made mistakes. Of course he did, but never the one of trying to milk the game dry. As a promoter and a professional player he sought to earn big money. But he tried always to enlarge the pool from which ·the money came by encouraging ever more people, especially youngsters, to become players.

Tony Trabert, the 1954 Wimbledon champion who later became Kramer's partner, once complained bitterly that 'Jack is more interested in his club and the bringing on of youngsters than he is in our promotions.'

There was some truth in this and yet it was not, in the long run, bad for professional tennis. Even in the second and third years of Open tennis there remained widespread suspicion about the professionals. Kramer's love of tennis always shone through all this and he, perhaps of all men, best retained the complete faith of amateur officials. Indeed, he and Don Budge were actually co-opted on to the U.S. L.T.A. in 1960.

It has not always been peace. Bitterly opposed to 'free loading', Kramer has quarrelled with most of the major associations about the sums of money they waste on free seats, drinks, lunches and dinners for themselves and their associates. Such money, he avers, should go into promotion, especially of junior tennis. He aims still to make tennis stars equally as heroic to youngsters as the baseball stars of the U.S.A. or their soccer counterparts in Britain and South America. There is no doubting his sincerity or integrity on this matter, and, in the end, the integrity has always broken down the animosities.

Possibly, too, this was one of the two outstanding features of his success as a player, the other being his 'camera shutter' mind.

Unlike the majority of players, Kramer never seemed upset by fortune. The moment one point ended – whether it be by a poor error, a fine stroke, a cruel net-cord or an erroneous line call – his brain shut it into the past with the finality of a camera shutter that can only operate again when the film has moved on. Never once in his long years at the top did an opponent get an extra point simply because Kramer was still worrying about the one before.

His integrity suffered and surmounted its greatest test at Wembley in the autumn of 1957 soon after he had guaranteed Lew Hoad $125,000 for two years' professional play.

Clearly Hoad's name had to be built to the sky, but when he made a British début as a professional his first-round opponent was Kramer.

If ever it was important financially for Kramer to lose, that was the moment. Yet if he ever suffered any doubts it showed only after he walked off the court after beating Hoad, then regarded the world's number one, with a masterly display of percentage, power tennis.

Literally speechless with rage for half an hour, Kramer finally told his friend C. M. Jones 'There is only one way I know how to play and that is to win. How much tonight may cost me never came into the reckoning'.

That, possibly, tells of the mind of a great champion and a greater man.

10: Pancho Gonzales

Wimbledon 1969, the first round. Pancho Gonzales, for years the world's best player, but now ageing into his forties, is drawn against Charlie Pasarell, an ebullient young American Davis Cup player. Pasarell had beaten the defending champion Manuel Santana in 1967 and the following year had taken the second seed, Rosewall, to five gruelling sets. Now, no doubt he viewed the prospect of capturing Gonzales' notorious scalp with considerable relish. It was fully twenty years earlier when Pancho had made his first appearance at Wimbledon and now, re-emerging from countless periods of semi-retirement, he lived in the hope that his matches would be tests of skill rather than stamina, for the durability of a silvery-haired grandfather, even so supremely talented as he, was of a necessarily capricious nature.

Rain washed out play all day Monday and it was six o'clock on Tuesday evening before the two men moved gingerly out on to the centre court. Personalities as rare and colourful as Gonzales are always an attraction, and despite the hour, a large crowd had gathered for the match in a mood of expectation tinged with nostalgia. Play commenced. Pasarell's tactics were obvious from the start. He crashed down his own services and waited for a service break, dinking back Gonzales' services at his feet and forcing him to provide the power for the volley. Once Gonzales was at the net Pasarell would lob and the veteran's precious energy would be lost chasing for the back of the court or jumping for the smash. But Gonzales' game held up and his fine overhead was able to put away all but the most shrewd of Pasarell's high balls. The vital opening net set continued for game after game, and, like two prizefighters locked in the first

79

clinch, neither man could break the other's hold. But as time wore on the break had to come and, predictably enough, it was Pasarell who took the set at 24 – 22. This equalled the longest ever in Wimbledon's history.

It was nearly eight o'clock. In the fading light Gonzales wearily groped for the ball with the eyes of an old man. Pasarell moved in for the kill. Gonzales was apparently unable to see at all and in vain he appealed to the referee to halt play. Three times his pleas were turned down – the conditions were playable even if Gonzales was not – but officialdom cannot make allowances for the handicaps of age and the match continued though by now the fuming Gonzales was keeping his participation to a deliberate minimum. The marathon first set could hardly have been any longer. The second could hardly have been quicker as Pasarell, unworried by his opponent's histrionics on the other side of the net, rampaged to 6 – 1, and a two sets to love lead. The referee, Mike Gibson, decided this was a suitable moment to adjourn the match. Gonzales, infamous for his displays of temperament both on and off the court, found it a convenient moment to show what he thought of the affair by hurling his racket at the chair of the unfortunate umpire and his tantrum continued all the way to the dressing-room. Some of the more vocal members of the crowd made their lack of appreciation of Gonzales' antics quite plain with a chorus of fairly hearty boos. There were a few other boos heard, presumably directed against the referee and in support of Gonzales as well as the occasional straggler who might have been protesting against the booers themselves or the lateness of the hour or just joining in for a bit of fun. In any event everyone appeared well satisfied, Pasarell walked calmly from the court and the bulk of the spectators made their way home, no doubt wondering what the following afternoon held in store for them after the drama of that evening.

When play resumed the next day Pasarell had had a good night's sleep. Gonzales, with a typical lack of prudence, had stayed up until the early hours of the morning playing cards and looked as if he was regretting it; but always the optimist, he had that morning told his wife, that he thought he could win. To the surprise of everyone, if not himself, Pancho restarted brilliantly. Possibly Pasarell had regarded the morning's play as a virtual formality, but the third set was proving as much of a struggle as the first had been and Gonzales, a huge man even now, danced about the court with an irritating lightness of foot as he strove to pull himself back into the match. Incredibly, it was Gonzales who got the break and Pasarell, after holding forty consecutive services, lost the third set 16 – 14.

As the fourth set unfolded, the huge crowd, packed to over-capacity, revelled in the unashamed brilliance of their idols. But in the eighth game Pasarell fell from his godlike heights and, fleetingly, exposed himself as a mere mortal with a tragic error – a double fault on game point – that gave Gonzales the break for a 5 – 3 lead. Gonzales grasped his opportunity greedily and served out to take the set at 6 – 3. Almost unbelievably he had forced Pasarell to a deciding set.

By now the players' box was as full as had been that morning's buses and trains that had brought the hurrying, excited fans to the championships. There was a queue that stretched all round the stadium. But most of those who could not cajole their way into the gallery resigned themselves to the fact that nobody in their right senses was going to come out except for the poor unfortunates who made their exit on stretchers suffering from nervous exhaustion. So the unlucky ones jostled in their thousands around the electric scoreboard outside the court and as each point appeared their roars would echo those of the more privileged inside who had witnessed the momentary victory of one of the protagonists in a rally of cruel, single-minded power or an exchange of delicate, almost fragile touchplay that became a glorious, refined torture for players, officials and spectators alike.

But Gonzales' legs were old and their strength was draining away relentlessly with the effort of each shot. Even before the end of the fourth set the match had become the longest ever played at Wimbledon, breaking the sixteen-year old record of ninety-three games in four hours and twenty minutes set by

Drobny and Patty in 1953. Pasarell waited for Gonzales to weaken : he said later, 'There was no way I could lose', and the crowd, for all their delight, sensed that defeat for Gonzales, even now, was inevitable. But Pancho needed no-one's sympathy, he would fight to the end, and, as a very old but well-proved cliché tells – the battle is never over until the very last shot is played. Gonzales was the perfect example. At 4 – 5 he dropped the first three points of his serve. Three match points for Pasarell. The crowd sagged, almost mute, and waited for the death blow. But Gonzales forced three errors from Pasarell and the match was even once more. Then at 5 – 6 Gonzales' service faltered again. It seemed as if the strain of continually serving to save the match had made the handicaps of age and fatigue into an intolerable burden. Pasarell threw up a wicked lob that hug tantalisingly in the air, the destinies of two men pinned irretrievably to its elusive flight, but Gonzales did not hesitate – his smash crashed past Pasarell and the fourth match point was saved. 15 – 40. Now a rally developed and Pasarell threw his killer punch with a flashing backhand down the line. For a moment it appeared that Gonzales had been left stranded, hopeless, a strange, beautiful animal dying in the middle of the court. But like some giant conjuror he had vanished into nothing before our disbelieving eyes, and then miraculously reappeared at the side of the net to tap a stop-volley across court where Pasarell's fierce, flailing arms would never reach. 30 – 40 Gonzales served viciously. Almost anti-climatically Pasarell could not control the return and the ball dropped tormentingly over the baseline. Deuce. Again Pancho recovered to square the set.

At 7 – 8 Pasarell had match point for the seventh time and Gonzales saved it again with just the showman's hint of a swaggering nonchalance born of habit. By now victory had become a matter of faith – and Gonzales believed he could win as Pasarell fought for his last elusive point. Then, in the nineteenth game Gonzales forced a break of serve. The positions were reversed and Pasarell, on the defensive, had to win the game to save the match. But Gonzales, even at the age of forty-one, still does not allow his opponents the opportunity to take victory from him.

He served out the game to love. Pancho Gonzales had finally won 22 – 24, 1 – 6, 16 – 14, 6 – 3, 11 – 9 and found himself yet another place in the history books of tennis and the hearts of his many thousands of admirers.

Gonzales has never won at Wimbledon; he turned professional when he was twenty-one and established himself as the world's greatest player when tournaments such as Wimbledon were out of his reach because of the fictional difference the tennis administrators made between the amateur and the professional.

But to go back to the beginning . . . Perhaps that Pancho Gonzales was able to become a world champion is one of the most surprising things about him. His father was a Mexican housepainter and Gonzales, born on the 9th of May, 1928 – christened Ricardo but nicknamed 'Pancho' by a schoolfriend – was the eldest of seven children. His early childhood coincided with the Depression, but the deficiency of food had little effect on Pancho's apparently boundless energy. At the age of seven an accident in the street left him scarred for life and by the time he was twelve the boy was becoming something of a problem to his parents. In desperation his mother bought him a fifty cent tennis racket as a Christmas present in the faint hope that this might occupy her son in a way that was both reasonably safe and socially acceptable.

But her gift did more than just keep young Pancho off the streets – it kept him in the Los Angeles public parks almost permanently. Such was his prowess on the public courts that Gonzales soon came to the attention of Perry Jones, then secretary, who had produced, among others, Bobby Riggs, Don Budge, Ted Schroeder, Jack Kramer, Alex Olmedo, Gussie Moran and Maureen Connolly. Jones was in an unrivalled position to offer promising players invaluable tuition, but he was something of a disciplinarian and Gonzales was far from his idea of an ideal pupil. For one thing Jones firmly believed that tennis should not interfere with his juniors' schooling. Gonzales, however, had different ideas. He did not like school, therefore he went as little as possible – which by all accounts was very rarely at all. On the other hand he did like tennis and played it with all the zest and enthusiasm of youth harnessed to a speed, quickness of reflex and timing natural to a born athlete. But even Gonzales could not progress very far without opponents and Perry Jones, banning Pancho from all official competitions, was adamant in his refusal of Gonzales' tournament entries – he would not accept a schoolboy truant and unless Pancho stuck to his lessons Jones would not allow him the competitive play that he so badly needed. Since neither would alter his attitude the stalemate continued and Gonzales lost the chance of free coaching – perhaps from Ellsworth Vines himself – over three vital years. During this time his tennis was confined, in brilliant isolation, to the Los Angeles Exposition Park and time off the court was spent lounging around nearby tennis shops and hamburger stalls.

Then, at the age of eighteen, and still without any real tennis experience, Gonzales went into the Navy and suffered, not without the occasional inevitable clash with the authorities, the rigours of military discipline. Fifteen months later, in January 1947, he was honourably discharged and arrived home only to be greeted by an ultimatum from his father who was rapidly tiring of his son's apparent laziness. 'Either go to work or go to school or leave my house', he said. Characteristically Gonzales got out. He earned his keep doing odd jobs in a one-room tennis shop during the day and sleeping on the sofa there at night. But it was not too long before his family relented and Gonzales was allowed home. Amidst this atmosphere of near-chaos an application was hastily sent off to the Southern Californian Championships and Gonzales began to practise, still on the public courts, in feverish anticipation of his acceptance. Eventually Southern California decided to let him play – even Perry Jones himself could not with any honesty bar a war veteran just because he had played hookey at school. Now it was up to Gonzales to prove himself.

The tournament began. Gonzales coasted through the first two rounds, but in the third he was drawn against Perry Jones' protégé, Herbie Flam, the National Junior champion whom everyone had regarded as the successor to Jack Kramer. Although the match took place on an outside court Gonzales' skill had attracted quite a crowd, but in spite of young Pancho's efforts Flam forced his way to three match points at $10-8$, $5-2$, and forty-love on Gonzales' service. This was the crucial moment. If Gonzales was to vindicate himself and all the ceaseless arguments with his parents, his school, and above all with the tennis authorities themselves, then he had to win. Three successive aces crashed past his startled opponent. Deuce. Gonzales hesitated no more. A disbelieving but rapturous crowd watched him snatch that set away from Flam and race through the decider for an $8-10$, $8-6$, $6-4$ victory. It was the beginning.

His triumph won him immediate, ungrudging acclaim from Perry Jones, who promptly provided him with 1,000 dollars in cash and packed him off to tour the eastern American grasscourt circuit. His performances were, to say the least, erratic. All too often he would defeat ranked players in the most sensational manner only to lose to an inferior in the next round. His approach to the game was reflected in his attitude to money. Even now he was very poor, but in travelling from tournament to tournament he rarely lost the chance to live it up, though this was hardly surprising in one so young. However, typical of Gonzales was the way he handed back ninety-eight dollars to Perry Jones when he returned to California. 'I had it left over,' he said simply.

But in spite of his haphazard methods, day by day, match by match, Gonzales was improving and his true ability began to show itself. He entered the Pacific South-West tournament and in an incredible run of matches defeated Jaroslav Drobny, Bob Falkenburg and Frankie Parker before losing to the invincible Kramer in the final. But Pancho still lacked discipline. He went to parties, often all night; he smoked, drank, and indulged his huge appetite till on occasions he was lumbering on to court at a ridiculous fourteen and a half stone. No man could really hope to win matches with that sort of training. But Gonzales did – though obviously not as often as he should have done – and throughout the summers of 1947 and 1948 he gained both experience and a reputation for his unpredictable nature on and off the court.

When the National Championships at Forest Hills came round Gonzales was ranked seventeenth in the U.S. L.T.A. lists and seeded eighth and last of the Americans in the tournament. He reached the quarter-finals and, as luck would have it, was matched against top seed Frankie Parker. Now Pancho sprang to life. His big match temperament and sense of drama produced an irrespressible display of attacking tennis that had the delighted spectators whooping their adulation as he overwhelmed the sober, measured consistency of his opponent's baseline play. He disposed of the mighty Drobny in the semi-finals and ruthlessly demolished the defences of the formidable South African, Eric Sturgess, in the final. No-one could have stopped Gonzales on this form and no one did. He took the title with a straight sets 6 – 2, 6 – 3, 14 – 12 victory – sixteen months after being allowed back into competitive tennis he was the National champion.

Champion he may have been. But at heart Gonzales was still the same happy-go-lucky, quick-tempered boy that had condemned tennis as a 'cissy's' game when he had first taken hold of a racket not eight years previously. His first tournament after Forest Hills was the Pacific South-West, where he had performed so brilliantly the year before. But the new National champion lost to Ted Schroeder who had won at Forest Hills in 1942 but had not competed there since. Even though Gonzales had been moved up to number one in the U.S. L.T.A. ranking lists his play was rapidly deteriorating. The public began to wonder if Schroeder was not America's rightful number one. Gonzales did nothing to dispel their doubts. For no apparent reason he continued to lose and to lose badly and before long he was regarded by almost everyone as a phony champion.

But in April 1949, although thirteen pounds overweight Gonzales struggled to victory in the National Indoor singles championship. His next stop was Chicago and the National clay court championships. There he sweated his way to the title and lost some of the less violent of his critics as well as most of his excess weight, but he still had not beaten Schroeder, neither before nor since his upset victory at Forest Hills the previous year.

When that year's Forest Hills event commenced Gonzales had to prove himself once again. As he and Schroeder moved inexorably through the field the excitement of the Press, public and players rose to fever pitch in their anticipation of the final. The match versus Schroeder follows a pattern of many later Gonzales' five-setters, for, then in what was easily the most important match of his career, Gonzales held five sets points in the first set, but lost it 16 – 18. Schroeder steamrollered his way through the second 6 – 2, and in the stands Henrietta Gonzales wept as her husband's crown slipped further and further out of reach.

But Pancho's fighting spirit and his volatile temperament with its mainspring of pride, though so often a liability, would not now let him give up. Gonzales swept through the third and fourth sets for the loss of only three games and Schroeder, desperately attempting to ward off the onslaught, still trailed by a service break when Gonzales served for the match at 5 – 4. Schroeder clawed his way to a break point at 30 – 40, but Gonzales, then as always, rarely misses an opportunity and he fought back to win the game and retain the championship. No one could call him a phony now.

Pancho repeated his victory over his rival in their next tournament – the Pacific South-West – and immediately turned professional, for a signing-on guarantee of $60,000 a year. It was 20th September, 1949, and at the age of twenty-one Gonzales' money worries appeared over. But once again, having reached a new peak of achievement, Pancho slipped back. His first professional tour, versus Jack Kramer, was a total disaster. Gonzales was thrashed by ninety-six matches to twenty-seven. This was not quite inexplicable, for Kramer, then playing the best tennis of his life, had years of experience behind him against opponents of the calibre of Bobby Riggs and Pancho Segura. As much as anything Gonzales' lack of training had now become a deciding factor on the professional circuit whose continuous one-night stands were as much a test of physical endurance as of skill. But typically, Gonzales' pride would not let him admit Kramer's superiority, 'I made the same money losing as I would have winning' he said bitterly to a friend afterwards.

But his collapse meant that in terms of the hard cash on which professional tennis depended Gonzales was no longer a big draw at the box-office and he was not invited on the 1950 tour. Not for the first time he became an exile. He returned to Los Angeles Exposition Park to improve his game near the hamburger stalls and tennis shops he knew so well and earned his living working in Frank Poulain's tennis shop – the one he had slept in years before. For four years Gonzales nursed his resentment. His savings dwindled, he separated from his wife and the chances of his ever making a comeback seemed remote. But in 1955, Kramer now a tour promoter, gave Gonzales an invitation to play a round robin series against a field that included both Sedgman and Segura; despite the opposition and despite his lay-off Gonzales won it. A year later Hoad and Rosewall pulled out of a deal at the last moment and left Kramer without an opponent to tour with Wimbledon champion Tony Trabert. Gonzales was signed for a guarantee of $15,000. Trabert was getting $75,000. Pancho's pride had been deeply hurt by Kramer before, but he could not now refuse an offer he considered little more than an insult. Now Pancho was hungry for success, hungry for money, as he played with all the ruthless spirit of revenge. Trabert was annihilated by seventy-four matches to twenty-seven and although Gonzales had only got the 'same money' winning as he would have done losing, this time he made sure he won.

After that, Gonzales crushed all opposition mercilessly – though not without temperamental outbursts that have had him smashing court equipment from Miami to Adelaide and heckling crowds all over the world though they still adore their beloved 'pancho'. His victims on tour include Kenny Rosewall whom he beat 51 – 27 and Lew Hoad, 51 – 37. Against Hoad, Gonzales demonstrated once more his natural talent and adaptability for tennis. Early on in the series he had trailed 9 – 18 to

)

the Australian who had realised that because of Gonzales' restricted racket grip, under pressure, Pancho could only go for winners down the sideline and Lew made sure he was always there to hit Gonzales' returns for winning volleys. But, Gonzales, in the middle of the tour, was able to make a radical alteration in the bunched-finger grip he had used for so many years, and, spreading his fingers out down the racket handle he began to slash top-spin backhand winners past Hoad and overhaul his lead. Disbelievingly Hoad said, 'Before long he was passing me cross-court with his backhand every night. Only a colossal natural player could have done it.'

Gonzales has enthralled crowds all over the world and a typical clash was his 1956 Wembley final against Sedgman. This is how *Lawn Tennis,* now the official journal of the L.T.A., felt about the game. 'Not since Crawford beat Vines in the 1933 Wimbledon final had I seen such thrilling tennis as that played by Gonzales and Sedgman in the men's singles final.

'Sedgman pinned his faith on the tremendous hustling methods he used in 1953. Gonzales was at his peak, yet for almost two sets was outplayed. Because his philosophy is to fight for every point, he clung on. In the end his power prevailed. But what a slender margin !

'In this match superb shots lost points; only the phenomenal or super-human were good enough to win them – and even these were occasionally returned with interest.

'Sedgman hit an incredible peak at 4 – all in the first set, taking five games in the face of Gonzales' severest opposition.

'The break for 6 – 4 was typical, Gonzales hurling over cannon-balls which Sedgman hammered back like lightning. That he even saw such services tells of an electronically quick eye. To hit them so hard and accurately was sheer black magic.

'Sedgman's speed of stroke, eye and foot defy description. His power was greater than ever before.

'His nose seemed over the net when he volleyed; yet he seldom failed to reach and kill the lobs.

'There was only one question! Could he maintain such a tremendous peak? Not until the seventeenth game of the match did Gonzales break service, and only then after a magnificent backhand down the line off a cannon-ball service. Repeatedly both men closed into the net, there to bang volleys at each other with venomous fury.

'Sedgman twice held point for 5 – 3, to be foiled once by returning a second service over the baseline and then by an ace.

'A slight relapse allowed Sedgman a love game for 5 – 4. With defeat imminent Gonzales threw in everything for a love game – 5 – all.

'6 – 5, Sedgman, and two double-faults for 0 – 30 looked ominous. Then Gonzales served an ace. The linesman called fault, and Sedgman gallantly threw the point. Tremendous cheers – what sportsmanship! It deserved a better fate, for his next lob missed by inches and Gonzales then served two aces. Down 0 – 30, Sedgman recovered for 7 – 6.

'Some twenty minutes had gone without a bad error when Gonzales suddenly hit an easy one into the net. One felt the crowd jerk back into the realisation that these men were human. It did not prevent the break.

'Two fantastic passing shots took Sedgman to 0 – 30. A winning volley and an ace made it 30 – all. Another untouchable passing shot, 30 – 40, double fault, game. Five outright winners to one error, a tally which typifies the quality and speed of this epic contest between giants.

'Eight – all, nine – all, the games mounted. Two line-clipping passes and Sedgman double-fault put Gonzales ahead 10 – 9. Reaching set-point Gonzales double-faulted. Another double then a fault, but Sedgman's return just missed; deuce. Again at set point, Gonzales was caught by a low return. A third set point was lost but at the fourth attempt Gonzales crashed over a brutal ace.

'The match was swinging. Both men had tired and the pace was now fractionally slower. This mattered to Sedgman, for it was his zip and verve which counterbalanced Gonzales' greater weight of stroke. His backhand, too, began to lift a little. Still a great shot by Wimbledon standards, it became relatively easy to a giant of Gonzales' quality.

'Nevertheless, Sedgman continued to battle every point of the way and did not concede the third set until the twentieth game.

'The tennis was still magnificent, and despite the hour over 4,000 onlookers stayed to watch. Indeed, hundreds missed the last transport out of Wembley.

'Sedgman, caught by many lobs, tired a little and was no longer closing in for his second volley. He missed a few. One felt he was beaten but he would not quit. Right on to the sixteenth game he battled, but in the end Gonzales' thundering services prevailed.' Gonzales won $4 - 6$, $11 - 9$, $11 - 9$, $9 - 7$.

Since then he had hammered all opposition into the ground, and before very long he began to 'retire' at what seemed like almost regular yearly intervals. But this incredible player has come out of genuine retirement to beat those who had supposedly superseded him. In May 1964, having played only one professional tournament in the previous three years, Gonzales reappeared in the U.S. Professional Indoor championships. According to the other professionals he had no chance – age, lack of match practice and the loss of the all-important desire to win would rule him out.

But in three successive days Gonzales beat Rod Laver, Lew Hoad and Ken Rosewall, all of whom were playing at their most brilliant best. In 1966 Pancho made yet another comeback with a dazzling display in the Wembley Professional World Championship where again he beat Rosewall before defeating the supposedly invincible Laver in a breathtaking final. If Gonzales at 38 could still beat the world's best and even at the age of 41 turn the Wimbledon championships upside down with that record-breaking victory over Charlie Pasarell, then it is hardly surprising that he has been one of the game's most-loved characters and perhaps its greatest-ever player.

11: Frank Sedgman

With the clouds of World War II enveloping Europe and the immortal Don Budge safely out of the way as a professional, Australia snatched the Davis Cup from America in 1939. Their grip lasted until 1946, when the all-conquering Jack Kramer and Ted Schroeder swept to a five – love victory which kept the Cup in the land of its birth until 1950 when a curly headed, smiling, 23 years old speedster from Melbourne won three of the rubbers which gave Australia a 4 –1 Challenge Round revenge at the West Side Tennis Club at Forest Hills on Long Island, New York.

Born on 29th October, 1927, Sedgman brought nothing but happiness to his economically worried parents, Arthur and Edith Sedgman. The joy was never greater than on their week-end outings to the Blackburn Tennis Club where, as a special treat, sunny little Frank was sometimes allowed to join in.

In between week-ends Frank used an old racket and tennis balls to batter to bits the door of a nearby garage. Its location may have been decisive in Australian tennis history because the grass in front of it was so impossibly bumpy that Frank never dared let the ball bounce. Because of this he became exceptionally sure and quick on the volley and this, more than any other factor, was eventually to win him the Australian singles title twice, Wimbledon once, the American singles twice, twelve of the world's major doubles titles (including the only 'Grand Slam' of the big four) and over $100,000 in the first year of his long and distinguished career as a contract professional with Jack Kramer.

One of the corner-stones of Australian tennis eminence is the age group championships which take place in every major town, region and State. It was at one of these that Australia's 'wily Old Fox', Harry Hopman, first spotted Frank who, as a twelve-year-old, chased happily and energetically against one of the known 'up and comers' Denis Lemke. Returning many shots that would have evaded even the best stars, Frank impressed Hopman so strongly that Hopman asked the parents if they would like their son to join his after-school classes at the famous Kooyong club. The answer was a firm 'yes' and from then until the outbreak of war in 1941 Frank was inevitably the first out to the courts each day – and still with that happy beam which characterised him from the start to finish of his competitive days.

Wiry but very small, he was equally enthusiastic at Australian rules football and cricket, but tennis was his major love and Hopman wisely ordained a long campaign of body-and strength-building exercises, many of them through skilled use of weights as directed by gym owner Frank Findlay. Enthusing even the dedicated Findlay with his zeal, Frank gained strength rapidly and as he grew, so he filled out, adding 18 lbs in 18 months to reach 148 lbs, his ideal playing weight.

During this period gym work became almost an obsession with Frank and this culminated with him linking with Findlay some years later after taking over the world-famous gymnasium.

Simultaneously, Frank listened avidly to all the advice fed to him by Hopman, including the unnecessary injunction to watch the top Americans at every opportunity. The influence of Budge, Kramer and Gonzales was on the so called 'big game' of strong service and volley, in contrast to the more artistic techniques of the best Australians – John Bromwich, Dinny Pails and Adrian Quist.

The essence of diligence, Frank was a perfect pupil who never ceased working on the elimination of weaknesses, many of them marginal by normal standards. Thus he was constantly changing a grip or flattening out a swing or working on his service action or adding top spin to his backhand so that volleyers could not reap a harvest of points against him.

Backed by his understanding parents and Harry Hopman, Frank made rapid progress but he missed selection for Australia's world touring team of 1948. Hopman, then a sports writer on the *Melbourne Herald,* quickly initiated a 'Sedgman for Wimbledon' fund and the money soon came in.

Though he failed to win any major singles titles on that first trip he gave adequate notice of the greatness to come in partnership with John Bromwich, by winning the Wimbledon doubles for the first time. Bromwich, one of the all-time 'greats', specialised in finesse and tactical wizardry. Frank, already one of the quickest and most aggressive players in the world, proved an admirable foil. With Bromwich to guide him he soon shed many of his earlier roughnesses and wildnesses of play and in one tour they became a team who would undoubtedly have threatened any before or since.

However, the main pay-off for those who provided the money came in January 1949 when he dropped only one set while vanquishing Bill Sidwell, Adrian Quist and, in the final, John Bromwich 6 – 3, 6 – 2, 6 – 2 to captivate the Adelaide crowds, and win the Australian Singles Championship. His win was all the more popular because the image then of Australian tennis stars was one of dour misery. Sedgman's sunny smile and boyish manner came like the proverbial breath of fresh air.

Now universally recognised as an inevitable world's number one, the only outstanding question was when he would achieve that pre-eminent position. It was nearly so in 1949.

The key match of that year, so far as Frank was concerned, took place on Wimbledon's court one against American star 'Lucky' Ted Schroeder in the quarter-final of the singles. Schroeder epitomised the all-out attacking game and was the more formidable because he apparently lacked any semblance of fear. The worse the crisis, the more bravely he played, as Frank was to find. It was a brilliant match in which the faster moving, better equipped, technically, Australian dominated play for long spells. Twice he reached match point and on one of these points Schroeder served, rushed for the net . . . and was judged to have foot-faulted. Back he trudged, his face wreathed in mental agony. Many lesser men would have double-faulted under the strain. Instead, he served strongly and again rushed for the net. Many lesser men than Frank would have missed their return, such was the tension. Instead, he hammered the ball back fast and low. Somehow Schroeder volleyed it back into Sedgman's court, not too strongly. Sedgman thundered the next shot even harder. Again, Schroeder contorted to make his volley. Thumping the ball harder than ever, Frank surely must have thought the match was his. Instead, Schroeder acrobatically volleyed the ball beyond Frank's reach and one sensed that victory that day was not in Frank's cards.

Perhaps if Frank had gone for a softly angled passing shot . . . Or had achieved greater depth with his second services . . . Or been a little more decisive with his volleys; but that was conjecture and, more pertinently, lack of experience. Particularly, Frank learnt the hard, bitter way never to let up because twice in that match – first when leading two sets to love, then at 3 – 0 and 5 – 4 in the fifth set – the young Australian felt the match was all over.

Twice more that year Schroeder beat him and then the tables turned.

By that time Frank was widely known as the 'fastest man on court in the world', a reputation the astute Jaroslav Drobny recognised to be true.

Frank himself claims that this speed was not a natural attribute and that he acquired it only through long hours of specialised exercises in Findlay's gymnasium.

Gaining in strength, stamina and knowledge, he began the 1950 international season full of hope and was not seriously threatened while retaining his Australian singles title. Then, with Wimbledon near at hand, he injured his wrist. Robbed of much power, he pulled back from two sets to love down to beat the clever American Art Larsen in a match interrupted by rain. He repeated the feat against Drobny but then became involved with Ken McGregor against Budge Patty and Tony Trabert in a marathon doubles which lasted four hours, 40 minutes and contained a 31 – 29 set, then the longest ever at Wimbledon. Both he and Patty were tired men when they walked on to the centre court for their singles final.

Undoubtedly the wrist weakness affected Frank but the major factors in his defeat were Patty's ability to make his strokes off a rising ball, to cover the net like a blanket, to volley with immediate finality and the poor length of Frank's services, first and second.

Moving in on the ball constantly, Patty was always at the net first when serving and frequently so when receiving. Match point produced one of the most exciting rallies of the entire fortnight, Frank twice forcing his way to the net, only to rush back in chase of lobs that landed plumb on the baseline. Finally Patty himself moved in behind the second of these, hit a strong volley and then, on the 22nd shot, blasted a backhand kill down the line well beyond Frank's groping racket.

The American Championships brought some solace for Frank and Bromwich captured the doubles but the single went to the amazing Larsen who, like Patty at Wimbledon, demonstrated how deep lobs can disrupt volleying attacks.

Preceding the singles Australia broke America's hold on the Davis Cup, Frank winning both his singles and the doubles to register three of Australia's four points. These included a 6 – 2, 6 – 2, 6 – 2 thrashing of Schroeder featured by the best tennis Frank had ever achieved at that stage of his career.

Still eagerness itself in gnawing away at personal weaknesses, Frank believed he had eliminated much of his vulnerability on the backhand and when serving. A lumbering, powerful American, Dick Savitt, destroyed this illusion while depriving Frank of his Australian singles crown. Goaded to fresh frenzies of activity, Frank slaved at these deficiencies and at Wimbledon was seeded first.

Raymundo Deyro fell to him 6 – 4, 6 – 3, 6 – 4 and Sven Davidson 6 – 4, 7 – 9, 6 – 4, 6 – 2. Straight Clark proved more troublesome but Frank advanced 8 – 6, 11 – 9, 6 – 3. This swept Frank into top gear and when he slaughtered Fausto Gardini

Pancho Gonzales

Lew Hoad

Frank Sedgman

6 – 1, 6 – 2, 6 – 0 and the defending champion, Budge Patty, was removed by the youthful Hamilton Richardson Frank's path to the title seemed comparatively clear of obstacles.

But, as the laws of mechanics teach us, action causes reaction. In the case to come Frank suffered heavily for his loss to Schroeder two years previously.

His opponent was Herbie Flam, who was making his first appearance on the centre court. His inevitable nervousness plus Frank's ultra brilliance began with Frank racing through the first two sets with a scintillating display of brilliant stroke making and volleying. Overwhelmed but brave, Flam struggled on and by means of some accurate lobs and non-stop, desperate retrieving stayed in the match. Adhering strictly to the adage 'Never change a winning game', Frank piled on the pressure but did not vary his methods. Lifting to the challenge, Flam contained all that was being flung at him. Frank twice moved within two points of victory but his poor pacing of the match and his lack of variety while not letting up, as he had done against Schroeder, eventually played into the hands of the clever American.

Clearly so near to the top, it seemed some tiny boost was needed to take Frank up the last rungs of the ladder. It came at Forest Hills some ten weeks later in a somewhat strange form, namely the more closely shaved, harder American ball which was so difficult to control off the ground.

In reporting these championships C. M. Jones wrote in *Lawn Tennis* 'So he's done it at last. Frank Sedgman, the pride of Australia and the man who seemed destined never to win a big championship out of his own country, finally fulfilled all the promise of his early years and smashed his way to victory . . .

'Sedgman was terrific. He found his serve-volley game ideally suited to the closely shaved American ball, which is extremely hard accurately to control off the ground, and reached an absolute crescendo of form in the semi-final and final.

'In these two matches he ran first through Larsen for the loss of only three games and then through Victor Seixas for a tally of six games.

D

'Sedgman, who throughout the meeting played the most decisive tennis of any man since Kramer, reached the final via Gilbert Bogley, George Ball, William Talbert, Tony Trabert and Arthur Larsen. Only Trabert was able to win a set and he took two with cannon-ball serving, decisive volleying and solid driving that sorely tested the Australian.

'Trabert's weakness was in his return of service and the shortness of his lobs but he was under severe pressure, especially in the second and third sets when Sedgman had every stroke working with almost mechanical perfection.'

Thus, at last, all the years of practice and hours of joyful application bore fruit. On the bumpy American courts Frank's simplicity and purity of stroke play allied to his acrobatic and immense speed aggregated into a composite player far beyond the skills of any of his opponents.

Against Seixas in the final he won 37 points with placements while conceding only 26 errors, 13 in the first set, seven in the second and a meagre six in the third. He compared more than favourably with Fred Perry, the last invader to win the title back in 1936.

Two weeks earlier Frank, partnered by Ken McGregor, set up a record which was still standing in 1969 by winning the men's doubles at each of the world's four major championships, the doubles 'Grand Slam' of Australia, France, Wimbledon and America.

There was only one position for him to end the year – top of the world rankings. In fact his top ten rankings during his best years before turning professional were: 1949, 5; 1950, 1; 1951, 1; 1952, 1.

Returning to Australia in triumph, Frank became engaged to Margaret Spence and their marriage took place in Melbourne on 30th January, 1952, 2,000 people mobbing the young couple as they left the church.

Professionalism was obviously in the immediate offing but a publicly subscribed £5,000 wedding present plus a sinecure job at a substantial salary buttressed his refusal of a £40,000 contract and enabled Australia to retain the Davis Cup, Frank again winning three rubbers in the Challenge Round contest against America.

The excitements of the previous year, the Challenge Round and marriage were followed by almost inevitable reaction and all his former technical weaknesses flooded back during his defeat by McGregor in the Australian singles final.

Drobny, then at his best as a clay court competitor, stood between Frank and the two major titles on that surface, the French and British Hard Courts Championships. Each time Drobny won their final, using the first set to lob every time Frank approached the net and so planing the last flash of speed from Frank in order to beat him over the latter part of each match.

Wimbledon gave Frank revenge, Drobny going down to him after winning the first set of their final. He and McGregor retained their doubles title and Frank completed a glorious treble by partnering Doris Hart to the mixed doubles title.

America brought Frank two more titles, the singles and the mixed, while he and McGregor went within a whisker of completing the men's doubles 'Grand Slam' for the second year running, Mervyn Rose and Vic Seixas downing them $3-6$, $10-8$, $10-8$, $6-8$, $8-6$ in the final of the last championship, the American.

His last engagement as an amateur was the 1952 Davis Cup Challenge Round, Frank winning all his three rubbers for the third year in succession, so gaining rapturous applause from the huge crowds at Memorial Drive, Adelaide.

There was only one path remaining, professionalism. The cable service carried his acceptance of Kramer's terms on 1st January, 1953 and in no time the Kramer organisation implemented the provisional plans already carefully laid. Their itinerary covered 90 matches in 14 weeks and involved an average of 250 miles motoring a day for each of the two cars that carried the full party.

The forecast was of an increase on the previous tour record of $248,000 set up by Kramer and Bobby Riggs, whose first wife, Kay, was the corporation's business manager.

Kramer finished the tour 54 – 41 ahead, both men taking the breathtaking sum of $128,000 for their efforts as players and Kramer a further, undisclosed fortune as the organiser.

Arthritically inclined, Kramer's major career was finished by the killing demands of that tour and he subsequently turned his attentions increasingly towards tournaments rather than tours, an inclination which suited Sedgman well, for he was always better able to gear himself up for exceptional efforts in a one- or two-week-long tournament than over a long, night by night tour.

This he emphasised at Wembley in November, 1953 when he reached the final and there thumped Gonzales 6 – 1, 6 – 2, 6 – 2 to take the then awe-inspiring £350 first prize. That, and a repeat win in the 1958 semi-finals, followed by a 6 – 4, 6 – 3, 6 – 4 win over Trabert, stamped Sedgman as possibly the finest 'money' player the game had known up to then.

Professional tennis moved him into the tycoon class and he should never need for money in his lifetime. Yet he remained always a games lover at heart and at the start of 1969 was in serious training before a bid to become Australia's top squash rackets player. Additionally, he applied for and obtained re-instatement in the tennis playing category 'Player' which, from 1968 onwards, approximated to the old category amateur. This reinstatement entitles him to enter nearly every international tournament. There is one last remembrance of Sedgman which shows he is the champion who remained in contact with every-day tennis and those who play it even at the pinnacle of his fame. It springs from 1953 and the Slazenger tournament at Scarborough when he was partnering McGregor in the semi-final of the doubles.

Reaching thirty-love on service, Frank served a double fault; then another . . . and another . . . and a fourth in succession, to give his opponents the game.

As a prestigious professional and the world number one he might have scowled or even thrown down his racket in disgust.

Instead, he reacted as he had always done, as a six-year-old, he batted the ball energetically against the wall . . . by smiling broadly. They call him 'The Gentleman' in Australia. Maybe it's an old-fashioned term but no tennis star in history has better merited that description.

12: Lew Hoad

Down on the Sydney waterfront they sacked two dockers for refusing to work. Up in the city harassed businessmen pleaded with obdurate taxi-drivers to take them to appointments. Out in the suburbs thousands of Hoovers were silenced while their operators glued themselves to the radio. For on that memorable day in December 1953 only one thing really counted, the battle of a blond, 19-year-old Sydneysider Lewis Alan Hoad against the ace of American tennis, Tony Trabert.

A nation's prestige was at stake . . . and also the finances of its Lawn Tennis Association, for on the gate money gathered by the annual Challenge Round for the trophy about which these men were battling – the Davis Cup – Australia's tennis supremacy was heavily dependent. Everyone and everything stopped for the radio.

It was a Challenge Round unique in tennis history. Twelve months earlier Frank Sedgman, then the world's top amateur, and Ken McGregor, who ranked third in the top ten, had defeated this same American team of Trabert and Vic Seixas.

Then the two Australians had signed professional contracts with Jack Kramer. Trabert and Seixas were so dominant in world tennis they ended 1953 ranked first and third respectively. Yet just before that year ended they were being resisted by two 19-year-old rookies reputedly far below them in standard when that year began.

The first two days had seen Hoad beat Seixas, Rosewall lose to Trabert and Hoad and Hartwig, a brand new partnership, fall easily to the smooth, experienced and well-drilled Seixas-Trabert doubles team.

Australian captain Harry Hopman, the 'sly old fox' of

Australian tennis, had been crucified in the morning papers about his choice of a doubles pair.

Suddenly, in this maelstrom of international tennis, sports politics, frenetic publicity and excessive patriotism, Hoad had to beat Trabert in order to keep the Challenge Round alive.

Perhaps fittingly, Melbourne's traditional summer sunshine had given way to a grey, overcast day suggestive of Shakespearean drama but the 17,000 fans jamming Kooyong were scarcely in a philosophical mood when Hoad opened the match by winning his first service game.

Captained by Bill Talbert, a former Davis Cup player himself and one of the game's shrewdest thinkers, the Americans had become expert in psychological warfare. As the players changed ends Trabert began the latest ploy – or so it seems to Hoad – by accusing Hoad of 'quick serving' – of serving before he, Trabert, was set to receive. Perhaps if Hopman had not been on court – captains are allowed to sit by the umpire's chair in Davis Cup tennis – Hoad might have been unsettled. Instead, Hopman said 'He's trying to unsettle you' and the effect had a stimulating, 'needling' effect.

Clinging tenaciously to his service games, Hoad was unable to break Trabert until 12 – 11 when, in the drizzle which was by then falling, Hoad outsmarted Trabert with a passing shot to take the set 13 – 11. It had lasted 65 minutes, a longer time than any of the entire three matches which had preceded it.

Gaining in confidence, Hoad increased the pressure, taking the second set 6 – 3. Then, as so often in following years, Hoad hauled himself out of danger with thunderous, untouchable service aces.

With the court slippery and both men now wearing spiked shoes – Hoad for the first time ever – Trabert's experience began to tell. Forcing Hoad to twist and turn, he repeatedly moved in to the net behind medium-paced, sliced shots which lay down on the court, forcing Hoad to hit upwards. This and a number of falls slowly eroded the youngster's confidence and when Trabert levelled the sets 6 – 2, 6 –3, few would have bet on an Australian win.

Tensely, Hoad won the opening game of the fifth set and then, forgetting for a moment he was wearing spikes, he tried to slide into a shot and ended up a crumpled heap on the court.

Then came one of those simple incidents on which history sometimes turns. Walking on court, Hopman threw a towel over Hoad, laughed, called him a clumsy oaf or something similar and the crowd roared with laughter.

Suddenly Hoad's tension evaporated. There was still a long way to go and he faced numerous crises. Trabert, justifying his world number one ranking, hit many scorching shots. Hoad hit more, one of them so hard he broke his racket . . . yet Trabert volleyed the kill for a winner.

But the racket break proved decisive. Without Hoad realising it, the gut had become sodden and unresponsive. The fresh racket he used gave Hoad the zing he had been missing. Leading 5 – 4, he reached 15 – 30 on Trabert's service and was powered out of the game.

Yet another service ace took Hoad to 6 – 5. Reaching love-thirty, Hoad menaced Trabert's second service and Trabert, seeing the movement to an aggressive position, double faulted; three match points.

Trabert, tired, served to Hoad's backhand and ran for the net. Repeating the pattern he had used throughout this set, Hoad chipped the ball low across the net, hopping and heaving like a man playing bowls, in his efforts to will the ball over the net. But the height was right, the angle 'impossible' and although Trabert flung himself at the ball in a desperate attempt to scramble it into play, there was never the slightest chance of him succeeding.

Thus Hoad suddenly emerged from the state of being a great prospect into the hero of one of the greatest matches in the then 53 years' history of the Davis Cup.

Cushions rained on the court, the umpire was coerced by the crowd into calling the score again, Lew's mother cried and his husky father snuffled a little. Prime Minister Robert Menzies beamed and a man yelled from the stand 'Give him a knighthood, Bob. Bradman never did anything like that'.

To complete the story, Ken Rosewall, the other Sydney 'Golden Boy of tennis', beat Seixas, and Australia retained the Davis Cup – but that must wait for a different telling.

Allowing for the emotion of the moment, the statements of Hopman, Talbert and John Crawford, another of the great Australians in tennis history, that this was one of the greatest matches in Davis Cup history – perhaps the greatest – cannot be discounted.

Factually, it resulted in Hoad ending the year as fifth in the world, a ranking that became four in 1954, three in 1955 and first in 1956. He would unquestionably have been first in 1957, too, but he turned professional after winning Wimbledon, and professionals in those days were not included in world 'top ten' lists.

From this personal triumph Hoad went on to ever-increasing heights of tennis prestige. Yet none ever quite captured the drama or immensity of this supreme achievement by a 19-year-old.

Yet somehow he had seemed destined to achieve it from the day Alan Hoad, his wife Ailsa Lyle – he called her 'Bonnie' because of her beauty and her 'cover girl' figure – and their three snowy haired, rumbustious sons Graham – they called him 'Kelly' – Larry and Lew moved from a small flat in Coogee to 43 Wigram Road, Glebe, another of Sydney's suburbs.

Bored with the move, Lew – then three years old – wandered into a backroom, scrambled up to a window somehow, and saw white-clad grown-ups playing a strange game on the courts behind the new home.

At that time Lew's favourite game was bunching brother Kelly inside an old motor tyre and bowling him like an acrobat down the lane. Soon one of the tyres was put to a different use – as a step to put against the fence and stand on while taking a closer look at the fascinating game the adults played.

When kindergarten began Lew usually took the long way home to have a peek through the cracks in the fence; he was well and truly 'hooked'.

Nevertheless, there was no chance to play until one set of school holidays had his mother really worried about Lew and his two friends diving in and out among the traffic on billycarts built from old boxes and scrapped pram wheels.

So Bonnie decided it would be safer if she taught Lew tennis on the courts behind the house. He was then five years old. For the next seven years he scarcely ever was seen without a racket in his hand.

His first racket was a gift from a local social club and was so loosely strung Lew called it his 'Onion Bag'.

No time for practice? Lew rose each morning at 5 a.m. and banged a ball against a garage door along the lane until all the neighbours complained about the noise. Sand shoes were expensive so he played in bare feet.

Soon old 'Onion Bag' became an obvious handicap but it took Bonnie and her husband over a year's juggling with the house-keeping money to save the money for a new one.

Little Lew progressed under his mother's watchful eye, but the family as a whole had one other typically Australian asset to give to their sons – athleticism.

Each Sunday, like so many Sydney families, mother cut and packed sandwiches and the whole Hoad entourage moved to a swimming pool, where they spent the whole day in and out of the water.

Alan, their father, was a talented, keen, all-rounder who shone in turn at swimming, diving, rifle-shooting, football and ice hockey. A fanatic about fitness, he put his three sons through exercises every night, telling them 'If you want to be men you must do your exercises and clean your teeth'. Even 20 years later when Lew was in the world's number one Alan used to take training runs with his illustrious son.

So if the Hoad family were perpetually hard up they were also eternally united and happy and Lew grew and thrived in the atmosphere of love and security.

When Japanese submarines infiltrated through the defences into Sydney harbour Alan and Bonnie evacuated their sons from Sydney to the country, pining for the day of their return.

When Lew got back from his grandmother his tennis had already taken on that easy, powerful appearance which was still apparent when he made a comeback on Britain's Dewar Cup circuit late in 1969 when almost 35 years old. He and a few other youngsters tried to join the Hereford Club. They were turned down – 'You're too young'.

Undaunted, they formed their own club and played matches around their suburb.

Aub Griffiths – 'Griffo' – a groundsman took over from Bonnie as Lew's guide. Lew began entering Age tournaments – tournaments divided into sections according to age; under 12, 13, 14, etc.

Though fluent, Lew was erratic – too erratic to be the top boy locally. Nevertheless, he moved up the various grades and by the age of eleven was completely dedicated to tennis.

A film taken when he was eight shows that Lew's service then was completely, perfectly grooved and different only because of his added strength when he won Wimbledon more than a decade later.

His Dad took him everywhere for varied experience – of surfaces, players and coaches. His was a life full of athletic activity, and then came the day when someone thought it would be a good idea for a couple of youngsters to play a 'curtain raising' match before an exhibition at Rockdale between Australia and the all-conquering Americans who had just recaptured the Davis Cup after the war-time break of seven years.

Lew was chosen and when he walked on court, scrubbed, shining and immaculately clad, he saw his opponent was small, frail and very dark. He was, of course, Ken Rosewall.

Lew hit the ball harder but Ken moved faster. Wherever the ball went, there was Ken to return it with the machine-like accuracy that later made him a firm place among the tennis immortals.

Most of the games were close but Ken always got them, no matter how hard Lew tried. Rosewall won 6 – 0, 6 – 0, and repeated the score for another four or five matches before Lew got his first game.

He might have become discouraged but, luckily, there were many men around who realised the differences of approach between the boys. So they all, from Ted Schroeder and Tom Brown of the American team, to Australians like Adrian Quist encouraged Lew to persevere. The papers began their eulogies, calling the two the 'mighty midgets'.

At the tender age of 12 little Lew retired. Contrary to the popular idea, he was not sore or disheartened by the defeats handed out by Rosewall. The Hoad family philosophy has always put defeat into proper perspective. Neither was he tired of tennis.

The simple truth is that he had run out of suitable practice partners and, anyway, at that age you tend to take it seriously when your pals tell you tennis is a cissy game.

He played Rugby, went in for athletics, sprinted, threw a cricket ball 108 yards, surfed, swam, kept fit and grew into a tough, husky young man.

He returned to a tennis ambience after passing his Inter-mediate Certificate examination – he must have been a genius considering how little schoolwork interested him – and began playing once more. Quist, mindful of Lew's tremendous talent, gave him a job stringing rackets at Dunlops.

Better, he fed him constant advice, especially about the mental aspect of tennis, and arranged regular practice. Dinny Pails gave him lessons.

The breakthrough came a few days before his 15th birthday when, on a back court at the White City and with everything clicking with the sweetness of a Rolls-Royce engine, Lew met and beat Ken Rosewall 6 – 3, 6 – 2 in the N.S.W. Junior Cham-pionship.

That night he met John Kleisman in the final of the Australian Junior Table Tennis Championship, just losing after two long games. There were many who said Lew could become world champion but he declined . . . the tennis 'hooks' were well and truly home.

This and other good results earned a trip to Melbourne where Lew began his first work-outs at Frank Finlay's famous gym-nasium, now owned by Frank Sedgman. This is where Hopman, who now took Lew under his wing, sent all Australians under his care for specialised training. There was coaching, too, from

Pat O'Hara Wood, a former Wimbledon doubles champion.

By then just turned 16, Lew was five feet nine inches tall, strong as a young ox and the most powerful server in the country. There was no question of Findlay training Lew for strength. Agility, speed off the mark, suppleness, stamina – these were the factors uppermost in the minds of those guiding Lew.

The 1952 season saw Lew lose his national junior champion title to Rosewall and in the April the 'mighty midgets' were chosen for their first overseas trip. His father and mother went out to Mascot airport – just by Botany Bay where Captain Cook first staked his claim for Britain – and during a somewhat emotional parting Lew vowed to himself that he would do everything within his power to make them and Australia proud of him. From then on, no matter what Lew Hoad might or might not do when entered as a private individual, when representing Australia he fought till he dropped.

After a few days training in England the team moved to Paris for the French Championships. Unofficially the world championships on hard courts, they are staged at the Stade Roland Garros in the leafy, Ritzy 16th 'arrondissement' of Paris, Auteuil.

The red courts have a clay base on which is packed red brickdust. The bound is high and slow, totally unlike the Australian grass courts, on which the ball skids through fast and low.

Completely strange to such a surface, Lew soon found himself against Eric Sturgess of South Africa, one of the world's greatest on such surfaces. A war-time Spitfire pilot, this brave, athletic Springbok moved with effortless ease and Lew met with the greatest difficulty in blasting the ball beyond his reach. Even so, he achieved a 9 – 7, 8 – 6, 6 – 4 score and European sports writers realised immediately that all the advance songs of praise were fully justified.

Two preliminary tournaments preceded Wimbledon and as Lew rode down shady Victoria Drive in one of the luxurious limousines used for the transportation of competitors nervousness began to numb his feelings. He was very nervous when he began his first match against Guiseppe Merlo, a small, doll-like dark little man with the good looks and dancing feet of a matinée idol. Merlo keeps two hands on the racket handle when hitting on the backhand side, uses a 12-ounce racket strung so slackly it made 'onion bag' seem board tight, takes each ball soon after it bounces and manoeuvres, finesses and angles with tantalising skill.

Lew played well and to the surprise of many squeezed home 4 – 6, 7 – 5, 2 – 6, 6 – 2, 6 – 2, a big win for a 17-year-old youngster on his first trip. Wins over another Italian Roland del Bello and the Austrian 'Clown Prince of Tennis' Freddie Huber preceded Lew's fourth round, centre court meeting with Jaroslav Drobny, later to become a close friend and adviser but for many years a bogy man to Lew on court.

Drobny gave little away, attacked wisely and won 6 – 3, 3 – 6, 8 – 6, 6 – 3. But statisticians in the crowd noted Lew's 14 aces and Drobny observed that in two or three years' time Lew would be unplayable.

Strangely, that match did not ignite any tremendous enthusiasm in the crowd. That came when Lew and Rosewall met and beat the second favourites for the doubles title, Dick Savitt and Gardner Mulloy. Both were tremendous competitors – scowlers who never smiled – and vastly talented players. The 'mighty midgets' began uncertainly and then, suddenly, erupted. The better Savitt and Mulloy played, the higher the boys raised their standards. Some of their ground strokes, taken almost on the half volley as the older men worked them out of position flashed like the proverbial lightning into seemingly non-existent gaps. They took a two sets to one lead, lost the fourth set and the crowd roared every time they hit the ball. Savitt, a fine sport, showed his enjoyment and appreciation of their wizardry with huge grins. Mulloy relaxed as he threw everything he knew into the fifth set. The break came when they raced back for a lob, Rosewall taking the ball from well behind the baseline and rifling a backhand drive with his back half to the net that sped like a bullet between the Americans.

Moments later they won 6 – 4, 8 – 6, 1 – 6, 3 – 6, 7 – 5, the huge Savitt seemed almost to engulf them with his handshakes, the seemingly angry Mulloy suddenly laughed and told press-men 'Great – those kids are great.'

It is doubtful if anyone who saw that match will ever forget it, for not only was it tennis at its highest level, it was com-petitive sport exemplifying all the finest Olympian ideals.

So Lew and Rosewall were suddenly world stars and adula-tion swept them onwards, their run ending in the semi-final against Seixas and Sturgess.

Clearly, only time was now between Lew and the highest honours in the game. With Hopman to guide him, Lew showed an insatiable capacity for work. Detailed work for, as he later wrote in Britain's *Lawn Tennis,* quality of effort is far more important than quantity.

No minor fault was ever allowed to grow into a major weak-ness. No sooner was it discovered than Lew – at any time and no matter how many matches he had played – would be out on the court with Hopman working away to eradicate it before the next day.

The nature of his shots, added to his youth and inexperience, inevitably led to heavy floods of errors. Beaten by Frank Sedg-man 6 – 2, 6 – 1, 6 – 3 in the American Championships, Hoad made 64 mistakes. Mercer Beasley, the great American coach, aimed always to keep mistakes below ten a set, even aggressive champions like Wilmer Allison. So Lew was making two or three times as many as he should.

This first tour was a regimented affair, with Hopman and his notebook always in evidence. Into this went records of the fines he imposed for such misdemeanours as swearing, bad manners, appearing at dinner without a tie and so on. Within the team it was something of a joke, with the players ribbing one another and calling repeatedly 'Put it in the book, Hop'. Yet there was no denying discipline was strict and when a lively journalist hit on the phrase 'Hopman's chain gang' it stuck.

Later, Lew was to find the discipline irksome but as a teenager Hopman on the tours was a magnificent substitute-father figure. No matter what other characteristics he might have concealed, the one he has never been able to mask is this deep liking for children. Lew sprouted and flourished under the guidance.

Yet when he returned to Australia his form was disappointing. This is a common phenomenon. Experience gained on a tour leads to changes of ideas and attitudes. Often they are almost subconscious. They have to be merged into the player's game and during the change his form suffers. Anxiety, too, inhibits most youngsters, for they are conscious of and grateful for the chance they have been given and are eager – over eager – to show their friends and benefactors how they have improved.

Nevertheless, Lew was chosen for the Davis Cup team, even if those 1952 post-Christmas days were spent as an anxious spectator in the Adelaide stands. Not too anxious, for Lew had not been a great watcher since his toddler days. Back at the team's hotel Frank Sedgman and Ken McGregor spent a considerable amount of time around and near Jack Kramer. Once the Cup was safely retained it surprised no one when, late on 'V' night, they announced they had turned professional.

Suddenly the 'wonder boys' – 'the Mighty Midgets' had died as a name – were thrust into the position of potential defenders of the Cup.

The main Australian season spreads from late October to the end of January and 1952-53 overall was not one of Hoad's best. Nevertheless, he was again selected for the overseas team which left earlier than usual in order to compete in Egypt and Italy. Perhaps because of the sensational début a year earlier, Lew seemed a little over anxious throughout that tour and at Wimbledon a slight case of food poisoning – kept quiet at the time – contributed to his defeat by Seixas in the quarter-finals. But as Seixas had beaten him in earlier encounters and became the Wimbledon winner, this was not an unusual result. Indeed, if Lew had been fully fit, it is improbable that he could have beaten the highly competitive, tenacious American. In America Lew won the singles at Orange but was beaten by Seixas when the two met in the American Championships.

This was a revealing loss, for on a hot, humid afternoon

Seixas 'paced' his efforts so skilfully Lew came to realise the importance of this facet of match play.

Jack Kramer, by then the 'Supremo' of professonal tennis, now had his eyes firmly on Lew and Rosewall but realised neither was yet ready. Lew was gaining mastery over his erratic ground strokes but there was still some way to go. Meanwhile, Sedgman and Kramer were providing superb tennis and producing the biggest financial profits in tennis history on their tour so there was no hurry. In fact, he did not sign Rosewall until late in 1956 and Hoad on the last evening of Wimbledon 1957.

Throughout the 1953 tour Hopman worked incessantly, on and off court, to bring his young charges forward to a pitch where they could successfully defend the Davis Cup.

This entailed Lew overcoming the 'Seixas bogy' and Rosewall, who could always handle Seixas, learning how to beat his particular 'Injun', Tony Trabert. Until this happened, or looked like happening, Mervyn Rose and Rex Hartwig seemed likelier selections for Davis Cup action.

The boys returned to Australia and the American Davis Cup team began their campaign at Sydney's White City. Whether by accident or sheer, clever design, Lew was seeded in Trabert's half of the draw, Rosewall in Seixas' – a pattern to be repeated throughout the Australian season. This meant the 'twins' could only meet their bogy men in finals and with the Americans concentrating mainly on Davis Cup preparations, Lew and Ken reached the final at the White City and again in Kooyong, Lew winning each time.

Perhaps fortunately in the short term but sadly in the long, Lew was now beginning to suffer muscle ailments which, later, shortened his career. His back gave trouble and, at Kooyong, his elbow.

Frank Findlay ordered a ten-day lay-off, and so Lew was able to prepare for the Davis Cup without any recent losses to Seixas bugging his mind.

As things turned out, Lew and Rosewall were chosen for the Davis Cup singles in preference to Rose, who Hopman never trusted when the chips were down, and Hartwig, who was brilliant but completely unpredictable.

The draw put Lew into court against Seixas in the opening rubber and it was almost an anti-climax. All the hours spent on court or round a table with Hopman had done the trick and with Hopman sitting in the captain's chair on the court, Lew was as relaxed and confident as any man can be in the stress of Davis Cup Challenge Round conditions.

In the past the irregular patterns of Seixas' efforts and his unorthodox shots had disrupted Lew's rhythm. In this match Lew jumped straight into an all-out attack, clicked right from the start and Seixas was never really in the chase. For the first time in his career Lew beat Seixas, the 6 – 4, 6 – 2, 6 – 3 score atoning for many of those past defeats.

Lew's feelings after the match reveal one of the reasons for his greatness. He felt a little sorry that Seixas had not put up a harder fight, an emotion met in many other top performers whose love of the game and pride of performance in it makes them want only to beat the best of which the other man is capable.

He was to need this attitude of mind two days later when, with Australia 1 – 2 down, he met Trabert in the match described in the opening of this chapter.

Victory for Lew meant the end of one era and heralded in another – literally. As Lew walked into the hotel for the Davis Cup dinner later that day he was handed his call-up papers for National Service.

Severe illness, probably the result of an insect or snake bite, marred Lew's army life but he left the service reasonably fit, thanks to tremendous personal discipline in his training. Lacking practice, he began the 1954 tour and is unlikely ever to forget Gardner Mulloy and the French Championships that year.

First Mulloy beat Lew in the singles, finishing the match with a dream backhand passing shot down the line. Then in the doubles Mulloy smashed a short lob with all his strength and the ball thundered into Lew's face. For a long while it seemed he had been seriously injured and there are some who believe his tennis was, in fact, affected for some weeks afterwards.

Wimbledon is preceded by the London Championships at Queen's Club, an unreal tournament in which no one really wants to go all out because of husbanding mental and physical strengths for the Wimbledon fortnight to come.

Lew won at Queen's, beating Rose in the final, and at Wimbledon avenged Paris by beating Mulloy. But his game was still forming and Drobny far too clever in the quarter-finals. Drobny went on to win the singles, a fine 'King Bruce and the Spider' effort, for he had first played there 16 years earlier in 1938.

Drobny hammered Lew off the court as well as on it, telling him time and again 'You will become a great player once you stop trying to hit every ball at a hundred miles an hour.'

Round about this time Lew suffered continuous criticism for his surly looks on court. There is no denying that he was a scowler rather than a smiler but he vowed then – and does now – that this resulted from the efforts he had to make in order to maintain concentration. Subsequently, his inherent good nature was proved time and again but then he was subjected to many adverse Press notices which caused him more distress than was realised.

He was also thinking constantly about Jennifer Staley, a noted Sydney tennis star with strong artistic talents. So 1954 was a difficult year and there were many experts ready to write Lew off as a juvenile 'wonder boy' who had burned himself out. By the end of the year he was ready to give up serious tennis.

This reflected in further on-court incidents, culminating in the day when he slammed a ball out of the ground and Jennifer refused to speak to him for a while.

During this period Hopman and Quist were great friends and advisers but he was not the Hoad of 1953 when the Challenge Round came and America raced into a winning three-love lead, Trabert beating Hoad 6 – 4, 2 – 6, 12 – 10, 6 – 3 in the opening rubber.

There was a better start to 1955. Although beaten by Rosewall in the final of the Australian, Lew was settling back into his old, easy-going way and when both he and Jennie were chosen for the Australian touring teams, the clouds really began to disperse.

Before leaving the couple decided they would announce their official engagement when the teams joined up in London. They went one better by marrying on the Saturday before Wimbledon.

The fuss that followed the wedding was scarcely an ideal preparation for the championships and he was no match for Budge Patty in the quarter-finals, Patty recapturing his 1950 Wimbledon winning form in defeating Lew 6 – 4, 6 – 4, 6 – 4. By now Hopman had split the Hoad-Rosewall doubles partnership, Hoad gaining some consolation for his singles defeat by helping Rex Hartwig to a straight sets win over Rosewall and Neale Fraser in the doubles final.

Loss of the Davis Cup entailed playing through the American zone and the inter-zone stages for the right to meet America in the Challenge Round. In order to house-hunt, Jennie left for home right after Wimbledon and Lew, more contented and settled than for a couple of years, travelled over to the U.S.A. for the start of the American season.

It was to prove the start of a 22-month spell which ended with the 1957 Wimbledon and a professional contract that smashed to smithereens all previous cash records.

His form began to peak in 'threesomes', a form of training in which two men hammer a series of balls against one in non-stop succession. Unless a man is in peak condition, five minutes will drive him into a distressing oxygen debt and muscular exhaustion. Hopman timed the build-up superbly, Hoad reaching the finest form of his career on the first day of the Challenge Round when he beat Trabert 4 – 6, 6 – 3, 6 – 3, 8 – 6. On the last day he defeated Seixas 7 – 9, 6 – 1, 6 – 4, 6 – 4 to complete an Australian five-nothing whitewash of the Americans.

Trabert gained revenge in the American Championships, going on to win them and end the year indisputably top of the world top ten rankings.

Despite this, the writing was on the wall. Trabert, Rosewall and Hoad were in constant demand by Kramer. Inevitably, all would sign as professionals. The only questions were in what order, when and for what guarantees.

Jennie gave birth to a daughter, the couple moved into a home at Parsley Bay, a Sydney suburb, life was hectic if sweet and Lew felt great.

So 1956 was a year of continuous triumph. With control now tempering his enormous power and responsibility motivating his concentration, Hoad slammed his way around the big championships. Rosewall fell to him in the Australian final, Sven Davidson, a purposeful intelligent Swede, in the final of the French. At Wimbledon he overcame Rosewall in a four-set final which reached great heights.

Only one more win – the American Championships – was needed to complete the tennis 'Grand Slam', a feat accomplished only by Donald Budge at that time.

Lew reached the final but Rosewall, profiting from Wimbledon experience, staked everything on an all-out attack. Clicking from the start and with Lew out of touch, he stopped the 'Grand Slams 4 – 6, 6 – 2, 6 – 3, 6 – 3.

The back injury which later played a major role in shortening Lew's career began now to trouble him but when 1956 ended he was clearly top of the world's amateurs.

The general public itched now to see him clash with Gonzales who was dominating professional tennis both with his play and his magnetic personality.

Severe back pain cost Lew his Australian singles title. There followed six weeks in a plaster cast. In Paris Lew looked good and then suddenly, when two sets down, a young Australian, Neil Gibson, went mad and hit the champion off the court.

It was only a temporary setback. At Wimbledon Lew drew French number one Pierre Darmon in the first round and overwhelmed him 6 – 2, 6 – 4, 6 – 3. Roy Emerson fell to him in straight sets and Mervyn Rose in four. Sven Davidson, in a repeat of the 1956 French final, carried him to 6 – 4, 6 – 4, 7 – 5, a score which in no way reflects the closeness of the match. Nervous, Lew needed intense self-control to maintain his form at the level needed to withstand the intelligent, powerful Swede.

So to the final against Ashley Cooper, Lew's last game as an amateur and possibly the finest of his career.

Cooper, the singles winner himself one year later, was helpless against the storm of powerful, unreturnable serves, smashes, volleys and groundstrokes which streamed off Lew's racket. For 56 minutes all that Lew had dreamed about during his years of intelligent, purposeful practice and preparation suddenly became reality. If Cooper defended, he slammed the ball beyond his reach. When, in desperation, Cooper made for the net, Lew rifled the ball past him before Cooper had time to move.

Lew's earned points in this final totalled 46, of which 24 were untouchable placements of one kind or another; the other 22 were quite unreturnable although Cooper did manage to get a touch.

Errors from Lew totalled only 29. Cooper scored 21 points on placements but erred unnecessarily 39 times. So of the 135 points played Hoad scored more than one-third with positive shots, possibly the highest ratio ever achieved in a Wimbledon final.

Strangely, he did not consider it was his best-ever tennis. 'Everyone plays better in his own country,' Lew said, a view not shared by Cooper. 'I've practised a lot with Sedgman and even he can't touch that play,' said Cooper.

Lew was to electrify many more audiences in his professional career but within 18 months the back injury took a heavy toll and in many respects his final against Cooper was the great climax of his career.

Certainly it had its greatest public exposure via television, world Press and radio, and many experts still cite this match as the greatest display of power tennis ever seen at Wimbledon, challenged only by Ellsworth Vines in 1932, Donald Budge in 1938 and Jack Kramer in 1947.

This, his amazing prowess as a junior and his heroic efforts in the 1953 Challenge Round are sufficient in themselves to ensure Lewis Alan Hoad has a permanent place in tennis history . . . in the affections of most of those who witnessed the unrolling of those halcyon days in the 1950s.

13: Roy Emerson

Someone, probably an American, once wrote 'Good guys come in second'. If every rule has to have its exception then Roy Stanley Emerson is the man who proves this one to be wrong. Born on 3rd November, 1936 on the 800-acre family dairy farm at Blackbutt, Queensland, Emerson first batted a ball around a court with a racket at the age of eight and began his collection of winners' trophies less than three years later. Yet he still maintains that many years passed before the number of tennis balls he hit equalled the total of cows he had milked.

There was a court on the Emerson farm and every member of the family used it. His sister Daphne became quite successful before she married the former Australian Davis Cup star Mal Anderson. He bears such a striking facial resemblance to Roy that the two are often mistaken for one another, a confusion of identities which they sometimes deliberately provoke for fun.

The family moved from Blackbutt to Brisbane, primarily because Emo's father (Roy was known as 'Emo' by everyone on the international circuit though he jokes 'it makes me sound like a detergent') believed his son possessed exceptional talent for the game and there was little work for the girls around the Blackbutt area. But, typically, he first called on Norman Brimson, the local coach in charge of Emo, to discover his true feelings about Emo's prospects as a world star. Brimson shared the father's faith and, since the Emersons were reasonably well off financially, the move took place.

Emo attended prestige private schools where he obtained satisfactory academic marks and attained exceptional athletic heights; at the age of 14 he ran 100 yards in 10.6 seconds and broad jumped 21 feet 6 inches. This athleticism subsequently proved his major asset as a world-class tennis star.

Emo followed the normal pattern of all Autralian Davis Cup stars in winning all the various age group titles at 12, 14, 16 and 17. His great potential was so apparent that he was selected for the Queensland senior team at the record low age of 15.

His never-ending love affair with tennis was, by then, deeply rooted and, seemingly, eternal. No youngster practised more assiduously or trained more intensively.

Even when he occupied top place in the world rankings many years later Emo was always the man who ran another couple of miles and then followed with 60 kangaroo hops while the rest of the squad changed and went home. His conscientiousness cost him many suppers but gained him the reputation 'Fittest man in tennis'. This fitness, especially the agility and speed factors, later proved his greatest asset on court, for his technical talents, though good, were possibly less rich than some of his Australian contemporaries.

His industry, determination and tenacity in match play zoomed him up the ladder and in 1961 at the age of 24 he won the first of the six Australian National Championship Singles titles that eventually came his way, a record. Despite this, his greatest fame came from winning the Wimbledon singles in 1964 and again in 1965. He seemed well on the way to a third win in succession in 1966 when he slipped chasing a ball during an unimportant point. Skidding heavily into the umpire's chair, he damaged his shoulder severely and although he completed the match, he was in no condition to withstand the pressures imposed by his fellow Aussie Owen Davidson.

During his career Emo has collected an impressive number of awards for good sportsmanship and his behaviour during this bitter incident showed just why; not by the slightest gesture did he reveal the great pain he was suffering.

This first capture of the Wimbledon singles stamped him as a true disciple of King Bruce's spider, for it was his ninth attempt. Perhaps because of this, the crowd gave him a memorable reception when his last volley evaded the reach of his opponent and best friend Fred Stolle.

Lawn Tennis reported the final in these words: 'Not too much was expected for both men are renowned for power and honest endeavour rather than super abundance of talent and the prospect was one of endless serve-volley rallies with few persisting beyond the third shot and many ending with a return of service error.

'This proved the case for the longest rally reached only nine strokes. Yet there were bright spots to relieve what could have been monotonous.

'Trained to the "nth" degree, Emerson set and maintained a cracking pace, not only during the rallies but also between them. On at least three vital occasions he seemed to change direction in mid-air, catapaulting his body like a cat to bring off heart-breaking – for Stolle – interceptions.

'Apart from his sheer athleticism Emerson's strongest weapons were his service and return of service. He reasoned his task was to get the ball back at all costs because Stolle's services are so speedy he hasn't time to reach a sound volleying position.

'Theory worked admirably and with Stolle obliging with 11 double double faults and three breaks for rain in the middle of Stolle's service games, Emerson won a shade more easily than 6 – 4, 12 – 10, 4 – 6, 6 – 3 might suggest.

'Stolle could have become dangerous if he had taken the second set but at 4 – 5, thirty-forty Emerson rifled a service into Stolle's backhand corner and that ended the brief crisis.

'Stolle hung on until 10-all when rain interrupted play for the third time with the score 15-all. Fourteen mintues later Stolle resumed cold, missed three volleys, dropped service and that was that.

'As much through reaction as anything, Emerson dropped the third set but took a one-love break in the fourth when Stolle opened and ended the game with a double fault. Dropping only three points in four service games, Emerson took another break to take the title which had eluded his grasp so long.

'Stolle dropped five service games in 25, Emerson two in 26, giving odds of five to one and twelve to one respectively. The points analysis roughly confirmed these figures.'

This moment of triumph came at an opportune time in Emo's life, for he and Stolle headed a group of top-flight Australian players who were then at loggerheads with the Australian L.T.A. over restrictions which that association had sought to impose on all Australian players. Because these players refused to submit, all were suspended from the Davis Cup team.

Although this did not distress them greatly as individuals, some, including Emo, felt the necessity of upholding the country's prestige. Emerson used his new title in initiating a peace move, his letter to the then President Norman Strange beginning with typical frankness 'On behalf of all the rebels' and continuing with compromise proposals which satisfied most of the players and gave the somewhat stupid association officials who had imposed the ban a welcome opportunity of saving face. No less pertinently, it enabled Emerson and Stolle to recapture the Davis Cup from America in the Challenge Round at Cleveland. Altogether Emo participated in nine Challenge Rounds, two short of the record-holding eleven of William Tatem 'Big Bill' Tilden.

Emo went on that year to capture the U.S.A. National Singles Championship, so winning three of the big four; his grand slam bid was foiled in France by Tony Roche, partly because Emo allowed insufficient time for adjustment to Parisian conditions. But, as always in his unblemished years as a gentleman and sportsman, he accepted disappointment without any trace of rancour or bitterness.

His achievements that year and in those which followed stemmed from a persistence and thoroughness which should hearten and encourage every 'scrubber' who has ever picked up a racket and tried to improve.

His early visits to Paris for the French Championships provide classic examples of his persistence. Raised on the ultra-fast courts in Queensland, his game was founded on pace. But the red clay courts of the continent are painfully slow and handicap such methods disastrously. So Emerson switched to safety-first methods for a time. These failed, so he experimented with different degrees of racket stringing tensions, hoping at first for better control and ultimately arriving at smallest gauge, peak elasticity gut strung to the tightest possible tension to give him sufficient pace off the strings to neutralise the slowness of the courts.

It seemed his experiments would pay off in the 1962 French final when he took the first two sets 6 – 2, 6 – 3. But aggressors seldom learn the refinements of defence and Emo scarcely knew the lob existed in those far-off days. Worse, Laver was aware of this blind spot and so he elected to go all out for attack, closing so close to the net for his volleying that his nose was almost hanging over it. As Laver correctly anticipated, Emo did not lob and so Laver won the next three sets and the title.

Far from depressing Emo, this setback merely strengthened his will to succeed and twelve months later he finally achieved complete mastery of Parisian clay courts by beating Pierre Darmon of France to take the singles. He repeated this feat four years later by beating Tony Roche in the final 6 – 1, 6 – 4, 2 – 6, 6 – 2.

His record in the American Championships is no less impressive, for he captured the singles in 1961 by beating Rod Laver 7 – 5, 6 – 3, 6 – 2 in the final and then gave an encore in 1964 when Fred Stolle was the victim 6 – 4, 6 – 1, 6 – 4.

Despite his immense championships record, Emo has never been held in the awe he deserves by his contemporaries and fellow internationalists. Maybe he is too much 'one of the gang'. Yet he would have it no other way. When there is trouble or difficulty, Emo is the first man his fellows seek out. So he does not dominate. Modest to an extreme, he has never suffered any illusions or false ideas of grandeur. After one of his greatest efforts, the 1964 American singles, he summed up the situation, 'I was lucky – all the others turning professional and after all the Davis Cup play I have had. I know how good I am and there is really very little difference between number one, number two and even number 20.'

This does himself less than justice, as a glance at his world rankings demonstrate. Ranked number one in 1961 – one place ahead of Laver – Emo's positions thereafter were: 1962, two; 1963, three; 1964, one; 1965, two; 1966, four; 1967, two; 1968, two. Then he turned professional and the top tens became a little obscured by organisational uncertainties.

Now a family man with a wife Joy, son Antony, born 29th March, 1963, and daughter Eileen Melinda, born 27th March, 1965, Emo's old loves, skin diving and photography, have slowly yielded to household activities. When he returned home after a world tour not so many years ago his first move was to mow the lawn of his Brisbane home. 'It's the best in the place,' he says.

His record in doubles is no less impressive because, counting the Italian Championships, he has won 17 major titles. Much of the time he travelled the world as an 'amateur' though, with typical honesty, he always called himself a professional. He was a highly paid 'amateur' and it might be said he took a lot from tennis. Those near to the game say that his sportsmanship, sincerity and honesty put back a whole lot more. Certainly more than enough to merit his place among the all-time greats.

14: Ken Rosewall

With a slight adjustment to the proverbial spoon in the mouth birth, Ken Rosewall, one of the great lawn tennis players of the post-war era, might almost claim to have been born with a racket in his hand. At any rate tennis rackets have been his constant companion almost from the day he was taken for his first outing in his pram.

Not only were his parents both keen players, but his father owned three courts at Rockdale, a suburb of Sydney. What was more natural than that the young Rosewall, who was born on 2nd November, 1934, should continually find himself being taken down to the court, so that his parents could continue their keen interest in the competitive side of the game.

Both played a lot of competitions, so that Ken became steeped in the atmosphere of the game from the start. When he left the pram and began to toddle around he was given his own small racket. His parents would play with him, but for long periods while they were involved in matches, Ken would be left near a convenient wall or fence and content himself by hitting the ball against this dumb opponent, which always made the return.

This was to prove the basis of the wonderful control that at the end of the 1950s was to find Ken Rosewall taking over from Pancho Gonzales as the world's professional champion until he in turn was succeeded by Rod Laver.

His father, who taught the young Ken his basic strokes, which have changed very little over the years, could not have dreamed in those far-off days that his son would capture every major title in the world, except Wimbledon.

Wimbledon has always held a jinx for Rosewall and it is his bitterest disappointment that he never won the game's most-coveted crown. He twice appeared in the final, losing to Jaroslav Drobny in 1954 and to his arch rival Lew Hoad in 1956.

That Wimbledon jinx was still to persist in 1968, when after winning the world's first 'Open' championship at Bournemouth and adding the French crown to it, he failed disappointingly against his fellow Australian Tony Roche in the fourth round.

Only in the doubles where he twice won the title with Hoad, in 1953 and 1956, can he look back kindly on Wimbledon.

The names of Hoad and Rosewall have always been synonymous in lawn tennis. Only three weeks separate them in age – Rosewall being the elder – and both come from Sydney. They were, however, from opposite sides of the city and were not the constant companions, growing up together, as many followers have assumed.

Indeed, they scarcely knew each other in their formative years except as keen rivals, who were being thrown together in the junior tournaments, where they had the greatest respect for each other.

Nevertheless, their careers were to run a parallel course with both, after playing their part in the golden years of Australian tennis, switching over to the professional circus.

Rosewall was the first to go at the start of 1957 after having won the American championship and helped Australia retain the Davis Cup. He was given a guarantee of £24,000 over 14 months and easily achieved this, going on to become one of the richest players in the game.

Wisely, Rosewall invested his earnings and today has wide and varied business interests, which give him maximum security for when he finally decides to retire from the professional scene. One cannot see Rosewall giving up the game altogether. He loves it too much for that.

It is this love for the game and a dedication which developed in very earliest days – even as far back as that hitting against the wall – that have made him the great player that he is.

Rosewall proudly admits that as a small boy he wanted nothing more than to be champion of Australia. He achieved that distinction in 1953 at the age of 18, but by that time his sights had been set higher and he was to march on to even greater achievements.

Plenty of youngsters dream of being champions but that's as far as they get. Rosewall left no stone unturned in his determination to get there. This, of course, is what makes a champion.

It has meant lots of sacrifices, but these were willingly given for Rosewall admits: 'I guess I was lucky, for I was always happy playing and never consciously felt I was having to make sacrifices.'

Naturally, Rosewall was given every encouragement by his parents and particularly by his father, who started to mould him from the age of five. They used to practise together before Ken went to school and would be at it again when he came home.

Carefully, Rosewall senior nursed his infant prodigy along, teaching him to serve and developing his strokes and, above all, encouraging him to think on court. He pointed out that because he was only a little fellow Ken would have to outsmart the bigger boys if he were to win. It was no good him trying to outhit them.

Even at the age of five or six Ken was having to learn this approach and his first successes were gained by waiting for the opponent to make the mistakes. Later, of course, he began to attack a bit himself, but even to this day Rosewall is not a net rusher.

Rosewall is only five feet seven inches tall, which leaves him over-shadowed by most of his rivals. But his small frame is packed with energy and power, which in his 'teens was to earn him the nickname of 'muscles'. He became the 'David who toppled the Goliaths'.

The family courts were sold when Rosewall senior went into the Air Force during the war, but Ken continued to play there until he was 11 years old. It was then that his undoubted talents were beginning to unfold and he was to move out into the world at large, starting of course in a small way locally, gradually increasing to cover Australia, and later all corners of the world.

They are far-off days, but Rosewall has never forgotten them and has stored up a host of memories.

He recalls that as a youngster his two great tennis idols were John Bromwich and Frank Sedgman. Bromwich was his first hero for he came from the same part of Sydney but it was not until Rosewall was 14 that they were to meet.

Rosewall's promise had been noted at the Schools Championships in Rockdale and Slazengers took him under their wing, giving him his rackets. His association with Slazengers still exists, with Rosewall proudly using their products.

That Easter Rosewall was invited to partner Bromwich in the tournament at Orange. 'I was so excited I would willingly have walked the 200 miles to Orange,' says Rosewall.

It was to prove a most successful outing for Rosewall.

Rosewall and Bromwich won the doubles and Rosewall reached the semi-final of the singles. Looking back on that match Rosewall recalls how Bromwich took most of the burden, but that he was able to learn a lot.

Rosewall's meeting with Sedgman was in different circumstances and a year later when he was 15. They were on opposite sides of the net. Rosewall partnered Ken McGregor against Sedgman and the late George Worthington and they were beaten 6 – 3, 6 – 4, 6 – 3.

Rosewall was indeed a mite among the giants. He was barely five feet tall, whereas the other three were all over six feet. He may have found this a little embarrassing but he has since become used to playing against opponents who tower above him.

What he lacks in inches, Rosewall more than makes up in skill and application.

His introduction to tournament play was shortly before his tenth birthday, but he had been playing regularly since he was seven. This was just another step on the road to fame and he had nine years' experience behind him when he became the youngest-ever winner of the Australian junior championship in 1950.

While Rosewall was building up as a discovery of exceptional promise at Rockdale, another youngster was creating quite a

Roy Emerson

Ken Rosewall

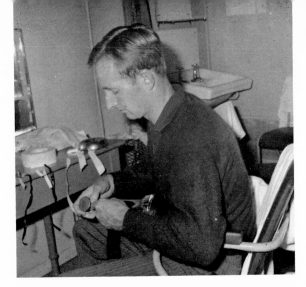

Above: Rod Laver preparing his rackets for a match against Gonzales. *Below:* Concentration and confidence: Laver in the 1969 singles final at Wimbledon against John Newcombe

stir at Manley, on the other side of Sydney. This was Lew Hoad. They first met at the age of 12.

They were invited to play in a preliminary to an exhibition between Jack Kramer, Tom Brown, John Bromwich and Adrian Quist at Rockdale. This was home for Rosewall, and determined to maintain his growing prestige he played out of his head to win 6 – 0, 6 – 0.

Rosewall also won their next meeting, another exhibition at Pratten Park by 6 – 2, 6 – 3.

Recalling those matches Rosewall points out that even in those days Hoad was a hard hitter. He was full of aggression, but lacked the consistency of Rosewall, who made up for lack of pace with clever placements, which led Hoad into error.

Later that season they met in the under 13 and under 15 finals of the New South Wales School championships and Rosewall maintained his supremacy by winning both.

Already they were beginning to emerge as two youngsters with the hallmark of champions and it was inevitable that they should eventually pair up for doubles. They came together for the first time in 1949 at the suggestion of Adrian Quist when they were entered for the New South Wales Junior championships. They were only 15 but they reached the final of the under 19 event, which they were to win for the three succeeding years.

It was a partnership which was to win the Wimbledon doubles of 1953 and 1956.

The combined skill of Rosewall and Hoad made them a big attraction and by the time they were 16 they had a large following wherever they played. It was around this time that Rosewall had his first big match against an overseas player – the American Dick Savitt. It was played in Sydney and Savitt won 8 – 6, 6 – 8, 7 – 5, 6 – 3, a score that reflected every credit on Rosewall, particularly as Savitt was to win the Wimbledon title a few months later.

The following season Rosewall was to take Sedgman, then Australia's No. 1 player, to five sets and reach the quarter-finals of the Australian championship before losing to Mervyn Rose over five sets.

E

With performances like these Rosewall had arrived. He was picked for the Australian Davis Cup squad in 1951 and in 1952 made his first overseas tour under the management of Harry Hopman. Hoad was also picked for the team, which was completed by Ken McGregor and Mervyn Rose. Sedgman, who was to win Wimbledon on that trip, was travelling privately. In fact it was his honeymoon.

The experience did Rosewall a tremendous amount of good, although it was not marked by any great performances. He was defeated in the first round of the French championships by the Italian Fausto Gardini, and in the second round of Wimbledon by Gardner Mulloy, of U.S.A.

Remembering that Rosewall was only 17, he was not unhappy about these results and the consolation was to come in the doubles when his partnership with Hoad stole the limelight of Wimbledon. The 'Wizz-kids', as they quickly became known, shook everyone by eliminating the American No. 2 seeds Mulloy and Savitt 6 – 4, 8 – 6, 1 – 6, 3 – 6, 7 – 5. They were eventually stopped over four sets by Vic Seixas and Eric Sturgess.

From England, Rosewall went to America with the Australian team. There at Forest Hills he gained his best singles win of the trip when he beat Seixas, but, as at Wimbledon, Mulloy once again proved too strong although this time it went to five sets.

Rosewall learned a tremendous amount from that tour, with some of the biggest improvements being made in forehand, smash and volleys. These had always been his main weaknesses and indeed they were pin-pointed by G. P. Lane, who gave him only seven out of a possible 13 points when assessing him in those prior tournament days.

That assessment had been a blow to Rosewall's father who was then coaching him and had taken Ken to Lane to see how he was making out. But the Rosewalls were not the type to be put off by a result like that. It made them work harder.

Rosewall's association with Hopman on that first overseas tour taught him, more than anything else, the value of physical fitness. Ken claims that it was in this direction that Hopman helped him the most, giving him the ideas that allowed him to build himself up at the gymnasium.

Most of the Australian boys used to work out at the gymnasium in Melbourne, but Rosewall was there only when the championships were on. He was unable to do the same amount of gym work as others, for a two or three hours work-out in the morning would ruin his tennis in the afternoon.

Rosewall contented himself jogging around for about half an hour in the morning, then playing in the afternoon. This suited him best, for he was in Melbourne to play.

At home in Sydney the training would be a little harder but worked to a schedule. He does not believe in overdoing the training, but he paid a lot of attention to abdominal exercises and breathing. He considers these are the most-important things to any tennis player and he has certainly not suffered in this direction.

When Sedgman and McGregor joined the professional ranks in 1953, after having helped Australia retain the Davis Cup, the way was opened for Rosewall and Hoad to move to the top. They took over a successful defence of the Davis Cup with Rex Hartwig, who played the doubles with Hoad.

The Davis Cup was at the end of the year and before coming to that stage Rosewall had made his mark internationally. He realised his schoolboy ambition at the beginning of the year, when he won the Australian Championship. He beat Mervyn Rose, who had now assumed the No. 1 spot, in straight sets.

This was followed by his second overseas tour, a longer one this time which was to take him via Cairo and Rome to Paris and Wimbledon and on to America.

He was beaten by Jaroslav Drobny in the semi-final of the Italian Championship but went on to win the French title, beating Vic Seixas in the final. With two of the first three major titles in his keeping, it was not surprising that Rosewall should be seeded No. 1 for Wimbledon, but it was an elevation that was to prove too much. Despite his many successes he was still inexperienced and the shock came when he crashed to Kurt Nielsen of Denmark in the quarter-finals. Rosewall had a bad match and it was one he had to write off to inexperience. He was still very much the base liner, allowing the opponent to carry the attack.

This was a failing that was to stay with Rosewall until he went into the professional ranks and sharpened his game against the skills of Gonzales, Trabert and Segura. He freely admits they taught him far more about the game and added the polish which was to put him on top of the world.

Like all tennis players Rosewall had his ups and downs, which must have brought him to the point of frustration. After winning two of the big four titles in 1953 he was to have a blank year in 1954, although this was when he reached his first Wimbledon singles final.

It all followed Australia's loss of the Davis Cup to U.S.A., when the full burden fell on Rosewall and Hoad. The pressures weighed heavily on Rosewall and there was no doubt that he suffered some reaction. He was still only 19 yet was the veteran of the Australian team that went overseas that year.

Rose avenged his 1953 defeat in the Australian championship, beating Rosewall at the semi-final stage then going on to become the new champion. Rosewall said goodbye to his French title when he was beaten by Sven Davidson of Sweden in the round before the quarter-finals. All this looked like being pushed into the background when he reached the Wimbledon final only to go down 13 – 11, 4 – 6, 6 – 2, 9 – 7 to Drobny.

This was an emotional final, with the crowd backing solidly behind 'Drob'. Rosewall played well, and given a little more experience would no doubt have pulled the match round to his way. The Australian says that he was not conscious of the partisanship, but it must have had some effect on him.

No longer the top dog in Australia Rosewall found some of the pressure relaxed in 1955 and immediately started his fight back. He regained the Australian title, beating Hoad in the final.

The Australians skipped the French championships and arrived at Wimbledon without the customary build-up from the European circuit. Rosewall blames this for the Australian failure at Wimbledon. He lost in the semi-final to that old adversary, Denmark's Kurt Nielsen, who in turn was beaten by Trabert.

On to America and the Australian sights were set on the Davis Cup. They made no mistake, crushing the U.S. 5 – 0.

Each of these overseas tours was under the management of Harry Hopman, but in 1956 Cliff Sproule took charge of the team. Rosewall once again lost the Australian title, this time to Hoad, who made the trip to Europe separately.

The official side again missed the French championships and Rosewall felt a lack of match play. Nevertheless, he fought his way through to the final and faced his boyhood rival for the title. Unlike the Australian team, Hoad played in Paris and was successful in capturing the title. This gave him the confidence to come through and win over four sets.

Although it was not realised at the time this was to be Rosewall's last appearance at Wimbledon as an amateur.

Jack Kramer, for ever looking for new blood to boost his growing professional circus, was beginning to dangle tempting baits before the Australian whizz kids. He needed them to inject new life and above all wanted to find someone capable of testing Gonzales, who reigned supreme as the world's No. 1 player.

Hoad was seeking the 'grand slam'. He needed just the American title to complete the quartet, but was to be denied this when Rosewall reversed the Wimbledon result and beat Hoad in the final.

Kramer stepped up the pressure and this time Rosewall found the offer too strong. He stayed in the Amateur ranks just long enough to help Australia successfully defend the Davis Cup, then started a new chapter of his life.

There was a double change of status for Rosewall for he had also married his childhood sweetheart, Wilma McIver. The added responsibilities of marriage and the security offered by a professional contract were perhaps the deciding influence in Rosewall turning his back on the Amateur ranks, a decision which was to upset the Australian Association who could see the cream steadily being skimmed from the top of their amateur players to the detriment of their Davis Cup retention. And remember that Australian tennis finances largely revolve around the Davis Cup income.

Jack Kramer's contract to Rosewall guaranteed him £24,000 over 14 months, plus a percentage of the receipts. This was a colossal figure but Rosewall is said to have achieved the original guarantee inside the first year. In five years he was said to have made £100,000 and he continued to go on from there although after the initial years of continuous play, flitting from one side of the world to the other, often as not just playing one-night stands, Rosewall moderated his programme considerably. As the children came along, sons Brett and Glenn, he has taken longer breaks at home.

Rosewall started his professional career at home in Australia against the renowned Pancho Gonzales, undisputed champion of the world. They moved on to New Zealand, then to the United States, with Gonzales eventually finishing the winner 50 to 26. A number of marathons were involved in the series, in which Gonzales was fighting for his position as the No. 1.

The gap between the professional and amateur was enormous, as Rosewall was quick to discover. He soon realised that his magnificent backhand, one of the best in the world, and solid control from the baseline were not sufficient. He remodelled the whole of his game in the light of lessons learned, improved his service and became more of an attacking player.

Rosewall's improvement in this hard school of professionalism was tremendous and by the end of 1958 he was running No. 2 to Gonzales. And this was despite Hoad having succumbed to the Kramer bait, joining the circus that year.

Behind it all was the dedication which has been with Rosewall since that boyhood ambition of wanting to be Australian champion.

He sacrificed everything to make good in his career. All his attention was devoted to tennis and when on tour his days consisted mainly of sleeping, eating and playing. His attitude has always been that the calls of top-class tennis are such that you have got to give everything to it otherwise it is easy to slide away from the top.

How true this has been with some of the other players who have lasted only a short while in this hectic turmoil of racing round the world displaying the skills everywhere. Rosewall has now been at it for 12 years, which surely proves his approach to the game has been the right one.

There is a mean streak about his play. And it is this which makes him such a great player. He is completely ruthless and gives nothing away, except good entertainment to the public. He has a much wider all-round game than others in the circus and this makes him a tremendous attraction.

The Wembley crowds appreciated this more than most for it is there that Rosewall has played some of his finest tennis. He first won Wembley in 1957 at his first professional appearance in England, then after a three-year break won it four times in a row, a record at that stage.

Rosewall was also very successful in the professional tournament at the Roland Garros, Paris. Paris and Wembley were the two major professional tournaments, and in comparison many of the other professional events were of the exhibition nature although money was the big incentive.

All this altered with the advent of "Open" tennis in 1968 when the professionals and amateurs were allowed to come into opposition in specified tournaments.

Rosewall had meanwhile lost his No. 1 spot among the professionals when his fellow-countryman Rod Laver joined their ranks after winning Wimbledon in 1961 and 1962 and completing the 'grand slam' of the Australian, French, Wimbledon and United States championships.

Naturally, it took Laver a little time to attune himself to the new pace and chasing of the professional side but inevitably he was to become king of them all.

Rosewall, however, was a long way from being finished. He was content to keep faith with his public and in 1968 at Bournemouth carved his own little niche in lawn tennis history by winning the British Hard Courts title, the first 'open' tournament.

Adapting himself much better to the damp conditions Rosewall had his greatest satisfaction by beating Laver in the final 3 – 6, 6 – 2, 6 – 0, 6 – 3. He played solidly to a good length, extracted full toll with his backhand, and was a worthy winner.

But Rosewall did not stop there. A few weeks later he moved over to the French championships in Paris and once again came out top by again beating Laver in the final. He had Laver running and stretching and it appeared that Rosewall had found a new lease of life. No man has ever had such a great span – 1953 and 1968 – in winning a major singles title.

With two such successes interest mounted as Wimbledon approached and it appeared that at last Rosewall might get that coveted title which had eluded him as an amateur. But it was not to be. Although seeded No. 2 to Laver he was beaten by yet another Australian, Tony Roche, for a place in the quarter-final. The strain of Wimbledon, with its long matches crowded into a shorter period than usual because of rain hold-up which put the programme 200 matches behind in four days, obviously told on him.

Rosewall looked very tired and dejected as he slid to a disappointing defeat in three sets. The Wimbledon jinx had raised its head again. There was to be another disappointing exit in 1969 when he was beaten in the third round by the American Bob Lutz.

Putting money to one side, Rosewall admits that he prefers life as a professional. He considers that the mental strain is nowhere near so great as in the amateur ranks, where criticism of defeat can be much more cruel and damaging.

At 35, Rosewall's competitive career must be drawing to its close. He has already cut down a lot of his activities to spend more time with his wife Wilma and the two boys Brett and Glenn, who already have their own cut-down rackets and may one day follow in the footsteps of their famous father.

15: Rod Laver

As his slightly built, red-headed conqueror moved forward to receive the 1969 American Open trophy and the $16,000 which went with it Tony Roche said with more hope than conviction, 'Maybe all that money will slow him down a little.'

There was little to justify this light-hearted hope of ending the supremacy of Rodney George (The Rocket) Laver for he had just completed the first-ever 'grand slam' of the world's four major tennis championships – Australia, France, Wimbledon, America – with the fifth, South Africa, thrown in for good measure. Probably there was no animosity, only friendship, for Laver, like Don Budge in 1938, ranks very highly among his peers of the current tennis world. Yet undoubtedly there was some frustration, for Roche had won five of their previous 1969 encounters, the two losses, like the third, coming in the major events where the stakes were highest.

But Laver had shown right from the days of his first world tour in 1956 – and before that at home in Australia – an uncanny ability to raise his game to unapproachable heights when the chips were really down. To raise his game through sheer bravery and concentration allied to exceptional speed and technique. And while the bravery probably dwelt in the genes which formed his personality, the other characteristics contained a heavy weighting of environmental factors. In these he may have been lucky but, in truth, his career suggests that Laver made his own opportunities at first and, when the Australian L.T.A. developed his potential, he seized with both hands and feet every opportunity to improve that came his way.

His self-help propensities became evident when he was still in short pants and his parents raised several kinds of mayhem over the destruction he was wreaking with racket and ball on the fence at the end of their family garden at Langdale where the Lavers worked a 23,000 acres cattle property.

Mindful of the threats to his tender regions but determined to continue with his tennis practice, young Laver collected some varied lengths of wood and suitable cross pieces and then went to work with hammer, saw and nails to build his own practice board.

His work succeeded better than many of his present-day opponents probably wish, for unlike the Laver fence, the board was rough and the ball rebounded irregularly. So the youngster received early training in rapid movement, so beginning an asset which many top liners rated highly during his 'grand slam' years of 1969 and 1962.

When Rocket was eleven years old the family moved 90 miles to Rockhampton, just north of the Tropic of Capricorn, where one of Papa Roy Laver's first operations was to build a tennis court to replace the one they had left behind at Langdale. Father, mother and all three sons divided their spare moments between fishing, back garden cricket and tennis but Rocket, sharing the fate of many youngest sons, frequently had to wait patiently till others in the family had finished before he could get on the court himself. Roy's family joke was always 'We'll send one of the family to Wimbledon one day and I wasn't really joking. But I thought it would be the oldest boy, Trevor. He was the one who looked good in those days.'

Like so many Australian small towns, Rockhampton possessed a local tennis fanatic – a former player named Charlie Hollis and soon Rocket caught his eye and came under his tutelage. It was a fortunate meeting for Hollis slave-drove Rocket, especially when teaching him the backhand drive. A left-hander, Rocket followed the pattern of left-handers by undercutting his backhand returns. This slicing technique is easier for all but especially so for left-handers; it seems almost to have physiological connotations. Hollis would have none of it. His experiences in top-class play had proved to him the vulnerability of strokes hit with slice and so he chanted, it seemed non-stop, through every lesson 'Get under the ball and hit over it – under and over, under and over.'

This was a crucial period because the action of hitting under and over imposed great physical strain on the slightly built Rocket. 'I would end a session with every muscle aching but the pain would be gone by the next day and Charlie would start all over again,' Rocket recalls. 'He always told me that if I wanted to be a great player I would have to hit over the ball.'

Even today Rocket is by no means a giant. When a boy he suffered a bout of hepatitis and so it was difficult then to see him as wiry and strong at five feet eight and a half inches and 150 pounds as he now is when competing in a championship.

Perhaps because Rockhampton is slightly remote or maybe because of his slight physique, Rocket did not receive any official help until 1956 when, at the age of 18 but only fifth in Australia's rankings of juniors, he was invited on his first world tour.

Beaten by Kurt Nielsen in the first round of the French Championships and by Orlando Sirola at Wimbledon, Rocket scarcely set the world on fire. But he did reach the final of the Junior Invitation Singles, losing to Ron Holmberg. Two months later he won the American Junior title by beating Chris Crawford in the final.

Despite this success, Laver was not chosen for Australia's 1957 touring team. Nevertheless, he reaped much benefit from 1956 though in fits and starts rather than through steady progress. But that was always his pattern of improvement. When the international scene returned to Australia in November 1957 Rocket quickly gave notice of his rising skills by extending Vic Seixas to 6 – 3, 6 – 4, 6 – 8, 6 – 2 in the N.S.W. Championships, a feat which led *Lawn Tennis* to forecast 'the match demonstrated admirably that Laver will be a handful in a year or two'.

The magazine was dead on target. In 1958 Rocket reached the third round at Wimbledon but there met his fellow left-hander Jaroslav Drobny who hammered him 6 – 1, 6 – 1, 6 – 4. Two months later in the American Championship he battled his way through to the fourth round and there held the powerful

Dick Savitt to 8 – 6, 9 – 7, 6 – 4. Then just turned 20 years of age, it was an implied acceptance of his standing that reports accentuated Savitt's strength in 'downing Laver'.

Progressing as much in strength as in techniques and tactics, Rocket began 1959 on a minor key, losing easily to Ulf Schmidt in the Australian Singles Championship but suddenly leaping forward when partnering Bob Mark to the doubles title. The signs were becoming ever more obvious.

This showed especially in his freedom from 'choke' or the 'steel elbow', two nervous tendencies which afflict nearly all players from time to time. In 'choking' the player loses all ability to hit, move or think freely. Frequently his playing arm and/or knees appear to be made of or encased in steel.

Usually he becomes tentative, falls into frequent and needless errors and often ends up tentatively pushing the ball back in the hope that his opponent will miss.

Then, as now, Laver reacted differently to crisis. Perhaps because of the harsh grounding in technique rammed home by Hollis, Laver's response to danger was to use his technique to produce even better shots and methods than in the preceding games and sets. Simultaneously, the adrenalin flow cleared his mind of all thoughts other than the computer-like thinking which enabled him unerringly to select the correct shot or tactics for the moment.

Still relatively inexperienced, he failed to make any impression on the clay court specialists at the French Championships but suddenly hit the headlines at Wimbledon when, in the second round, he eliminated Kurt Nielsen, the seventh seed, without loss of a set. Nielsen holds a unique place in Wimbledon for he twice reached the singles final, in 1953 and 1955, as an unseeded player. His strength lay in a lightning service and strong volleys. Laver's sense of sheer tennis proved vital and, added to his exceptional speed, this enabled him to stand closer in than most men and still have time to hammer back Nielsen's cannon-balls with almost contemptuous ease.

This hurdle safely negotiated, he swept through to the semifinal, in which he met the six foot three inch American powerhouse Barry Mackay, the favourite for the title following his showing in the Italian Championships.

Similar in many ways to Nielsen, but with sounder technique on the forehand, he thrashed over thunderbolt services at Laver for five sets but never intimidated or made apprehensive the little left-hander. Their five sets took 87 games to decide. Mackay led 3 – 1 in the fifth set when Laver's amazing hitting on the run turned the flow.

Bravery plus speed and good technique had brought Laver to the final possibly one or two years before he was ready for it. For once slightly nervous, he looked tactically raw against the Peruvian America had adopted for their Davis Cup team, Alexandro Olmedo. Relaxed, strong and more experienced than the youthful Queenslander, Olmedo won in three straight sets but admitted later 'I cannot say I felt exactly comfortable.'

Winning the mixed doubles and reaching the final of the men's doubles completed a formidable fortnight for Laver yet, somehow, his full genius escaped most of the critics, perhaps because of the controversy still surrounding America's use of Olmedo in the Davis Cup and Olmedo's approaching career as a professional.

Moving to America, Laver found the courts and climate at Forest Hills unsuitable to his game and physique and he lost to Holmberg in the quarter-finals in a repeat of their junior final at Wimbledon two years earlier.

At that time Neale Fraser and Roy Emerson headed Australian tennis but the 'Old Fox' Harry Hopman always went along with talent, especially when it was allied to the type of industry inherent in Laver. So he chose Laver in preference to Emerson for the Davis Cup Challenge Round at Forest Hills. Though he lost to Mackay, he put up a better fight against Olmedo than at Wimbledon, confirming his oft-stated view that progress came to him in fits and starts rather than in a steady stream. Despite Laver's two defeats, Australia regained the Davis Cup, Fraser thoroughly deserving the adulation heaped on him by his fellow countrymen.

The Australian State Championships evolved into a Fraser-

Emerson private war but the 1960 National Championships were staged at Brisbane and no Queenslander had won the singles title for 30 years. How much effect this had on Laver is difficult to assess. What is beyond dispute is the bravery he displayed while overcoming Fraser in a three-and-a-half hours final in which Fraser led by two sets to love and held a match point. In the semi-finals Laver recovered from a 2 – 5 deficit in the fifth set to beat Emerson, so he truly won the title the hard way. Yet with disarming and sincere modesty he said after beating Fraser, 'I did not think I stood a ghost of a chance when Neale led me two sets to nil but I kept on trying. Neale was very unlucky to lose. All the luck was on my side today.'

Two further insights to Laver's character arose during the French Championships where he met with enormous difficulty in overcoming Andrez Licis who held a match point. Till that moment in time his answer to net attacks had always been a fast passing shot. Suddenly he tore across the court, just reached Licis' return and hoisted a fast, heavily spun lob which completely surprised Licis, leaving him completely flat-footed.

During the Paris fortnight he was unusually quiet and seemed to be in pain though he made light of it. Luckily the team manager, Adrian Quist, was also Laver's boss in the Dunlop Sports Company and, better, a man experienced with young Australians. Quist despatched Laver to a specialist who discovered he had been playing with a chipped bone in his back, probably a relic of childhood. There was only one answer, a rest until the pain departed. Commented Quist, 'If I hadn't known him so well he might still be suffering. These country boys expect to work things off. They will play with an aching arm until it drops off and then try to fix it instead of catching the trouble in time.'

At Wimbledon he again reached the singles final where he met the experienced Fraser who was nearing his greatest ambition, to win the singles. In the Australian final Laver eventually scraped home through a weakness in Fraser's backhand defences. This taught the older man a great deal and in the intervening period he worked ceaselessly to eradicate this vulnerable spot in his game. Laver, recalling Brisbane, directed his attacks to the backhand, only to be met with a carefully pre-conceived defence that included many deep and deceptive lobs. He again won the mixed doubles but he and Bob Mark lost a thriller to Ralston and Osuna in the men's doubles semi-finals.

Fraser's tactics were even more effective when the two men met in the final of the American Championship, for they had been proved at Wimbledon. This was definitely Fraser's year but Laver was hard on his heels, their respective rankings being one and two. Nevertheless, this was Fraser's swan song. He slipped completely from the world's top ten in 1961, reappeared at four in 1962 and thereafter departed from the world scene as a top ten competitor.

Laver seemed certain to succeed him but the year 1961 began badly, a badly sprained wrist probably costing him the Australian title to Emerson in the final.

So bad was the sprain that Laver, ever game, played the round of last sixteen with his wrist in improvised splints. He then said, 'What happens from now on is in the lap of the Gods.' In fact his wrist improved and he refused staunchly to use it as an alibi.

Paris again proved a stumbling block, Manuel Santana's guile and spins finally baffling him in the fifth set of their French Championships semi-final.

Four weeks later his long rein as the world's best player began at Wimbledon. He was now nearing his 23rd birthday, was stronger, experienced and sure of himself tactically. The strains and other injuries which had been such a handicap over the preceding period came under control and he began the singles in a relaxed, confident mood. Pierre Darmon, against whom he always met difficulties, carried him to five sets in the second round, a feat repeated by Wilhelm Bungert in the third; Bungert was always inspired by Wimbledon.

Then came Bob Hewitt, Luis Ayala, Ramanathan Krishnan and, in the final, Chuck McKinley. Not one set could they muster between them, Krishnan's 8 – 6 proving the worst of the twelve Laver won. Krishnan, one of the craftiest players ever to grace the centre court, paid handsome and shrewd tribute to Laver's prowess when explaining that he is so fluent he is able to change direction of shot with last-moment flicks of the wrist and that makes him extremely difficult to 'pick', a sentiment dozens have since shared when moving in the apparently right direction, only to be passed as clean as a whistle when the ball has sped unexpectedly the other, surprise, way.

The American Championship again eluded him, Emerson winning their final with comparative ease. Even more than the slow, clay courts of Paris, the bumpy grass and humid conditions of Forest Hills always imposed a great handicap on the slightly built Laver, and that physical strain was accentuated by the strain of the Wimbledon fortnight and the period which follows it. In all the years between 1961 and 1969 Laver only won those two championships, twice each, in 1962 and 1969, the years of his 'grand slams'.

This, perhaps, is strong evidence that the brand of excellence which Laver produces for major occasions is not culled up without great cost to his mental and physical stamina. Certainly after winning the first Wimbledon Open in 1968 Laver warned a friend not to back him for the American Open two months later. He was spent, desperately needed a rest and knew that between the end of that rest and the start of the American Open he could not regain 100 per cent match tightness. Even the $14,000 first prize could not overcome the natural handicap.

Disappointed by his failure though happy for his friend, Emo, Laver returned to Australia, cleared up a few minor weaknesses which had crept into his game and made known his plans after winning the New South Wales Championship shortly before Christmas. 'I want to win the Australian, French, Wimbledon and United States championships in one year,' he confessed. 'Only one player has ever achieved the feat – America's Don Budge.'

Climaxing a brilliant Australian season, he duly captured the first of the four by beating Emerson 8 – 6, 0 – 6, 6 – 4, 6 – 4 in the final but, ever a 100 per cent sportsman, his joy was tempered by the knowledge that rain earlier had forced Emerson to contest five matches and 16 sets on the Saturday and the Sunday's rest had been insufficient for full recovery. 'It was unfair that Emo had to play the final right after his other gruelling matches,' he lamented, 'he has had the legs run right off him the past couple of days.' Predictably, Emo would have none of it, saying 'Rocket was just too good.'

The second hurdle promised to be the stiffest and Laver began concentrating on it immediately, so giving himself four months to develop his clay court game. Primarily it was a case of learning to manoeuvre and finesse and to hit to depth, and when he beat Emo in the five sets final of the Italian Championship and then paired with Neale Fraser to take the doubles he was clearly capable of winning in Paris.

He did, but what an adventure it was. Dropping a set apiece to Pickard and Jacobini, he met Martin Mulligan in the centre court quarter-final with yet another of the handicaps which seemed to plague his amateur days. Playing Jacobini he fell heavily and almost tore off his thumbnail. Terrible soreness put a virtual end to his top-spin backhand for several rounds. And that was a shot Laver knew he would need desperately against such a fast moving, skilful clay court expert as Mulligan.

Utterly purposeful and determined, Mulligan imposed one of the best-disciplined attacks seen for years in Paris against Laver's handicapped backhand. Judging the pace perfectly, Mulligan neither hit so hard that Laver could use the pace nor so slowly that Laver could adjust his grip and then hit heavily without feeling pain.

Mulligan reached match point in the fourth set with Laver serving but, as always in a crisis, Laver's adrenalin flowed freely, clearing both his brain and his muscles for action.

Quelling the emotional call to go for an ace, Laver served at three-quarter pace to Mulligan's stronger backhand wing, raced for the net and positioned himself perfectly to speed a backhand volley across the court far wide of Mulligan's scampering feet and groping racket.

What were those clear thoughts? 'Mulligan had been return-ing all my services down the line so I took a chance that he

would do so this time' he revealed to writer C. M. Jones later :
'If he had gone across the court I would have been in deep
trouble.' But he also showed himself not completely free from
the emotional, superstitious tendencies of lesser mortals.

Down to two sets to love against Emerson in the final and,
again, 0 – 3 down in the fourth set, Laver looked on his way to
defeat. Once more his combination of bravery and tactical
shrewdness prevailed.

Recalling the final in *Lawn Tennis,* he wrote 'When you are
two sets down against players like Emerson you need more than
good play to pull you through. I was lucky. But I felt I was
fated to win the Championship when I beat Mulligan after he
had held match point.

'Against Emerson I felt very near to defeat for an hour but I
held on hoping for a break. I like to begin slowly and get all
my shots working. Then I can go faster later on. If I begin with
a rush my game stays jerky and I am terrible.

'I thought Emerson began very well. He is so quick it is
very hard to pass him. I kept changing my racket every three or
four games and it was a long time before I found one to stick to.

'But I first realised in Palermo that no one can hurt me on
hard courts any more; Sirola told me after I had beaten Fletcher
and him and that has made me more confident.

'When you are nearly beaten it is no good waiting for the
other fellow to make a mistake. You might as well have a go
and force him to do something. I feel I have more control now
and know what I am trying to do.

'I closed right into the net for my second volleys. Emerson
doesn't lob much and so I chanced it. I knew I was behind but
did not look at the score. If I had know it was 3 – 0 I might
have lost. When I won the first point of the fifth set it suddenly
flashed in my mind that I was leading; I promptly lost the next
three. I could hardly believe it when I won the last point. I
never really thought I was on top.'

Laver saw the Mulligan incident as an omen. He never said
how he regarded one crucial spell lasting three minutes when he
met Manuel Santana in the Wimbledon quarter-finals four

weeks and one day later.

They came when Santana was leading by a set and 5 – 4, Laver having recovered from 1 – 5. Serving and trailing love-thirty, Laver was baffled by a sharply dipping lob. His wild swing caught the ball on the racket handle and it went in for a winner.

Serving again, he raced in and Santana flashed the ball at the sideline. With his back half to the net the diving Laver half volleyed the ball at a 45 degrees angle for another clean winner which Santana could scarce believe.

Reaching set point despite this, Santana made for the net and established a strong position. Racing across the court, Laver hit the ball as hard as he could straight at Santana. The pace and a last-moment dip baffled Santana and he muffed the volley.

Worse, for Santana, was to come in the guise of two net cords, the second of which never looked like crawling over until it plopped down on Santana's side of the net. This was more than flesh and blood could stand. Santana held on gamely but Laver, obviously, thought it simply wasn't in the cards for him to lose this one. So he raised his game to a level not seen since Hoad had thrashed Ashley Cooper in 1957 and went on to take the title without further loss of a set. Fraser and Mulligan, both of whom had carried him the full distance in France, made very little impression in the last two rounds.

Three down, one to go . . . But what a one. Appalled by the slow fall away of the American Championships, Gladys Heldman, Editor of *World Tennis,* and a group of tennis lovers went into action to restore the 'Nationals' to their former greatness. Chartering an airliner, they flew over from Europe some 70 of the best continental players and accommodated and entertained them with enormous flair and generosity. So the competition was fiercer than for many years. However, the operation provided Laver with one asset, his understanding friend John Mac-Donald, the New Zealand Davis Cup player who has lived many years in England.

Instead of being left more or less to his own devices, Laver was able to spend relaxed evenings watching television with only occasional reference to tennis.

The evening of his match with Froehling provides a good example. As the cowboys chased the Injuns Laver said, 'I was hitting the high ones out today.' 'You must get over them more' MacDonald suggested. 'Yes, I must get over them more,' Laver echoed . . . And that was the limit of the evening's tennis talk. Perhaps because of the company and maybe through a little inspiration gained from a practice session with Donald Budge, the only man at that moment to have completed the 'grand slam', Laver remained in great fettle throughout the championships and Budge said on television, 'After practising with Rocket the other day I am afraid that at long last my record is going to be toppled.'

He was a good prophet. Apart from Froehling's service and the second half of the final against Emerson, Laver never looked in the slightest difficulty.

Pleased with his form in the earlier rounds, Emerson analysed before the final that victory would probably go to the man who got away to the quickest start . . . And he had been friends with Laver for so many years that he doubtlessly believed that he would be that man.

But with the chance of history so near Laver abandoned his usual quiet start and jumped straight into a terrific series of attacks which even Emerson's great heart and speed could not cope with.

Rafael Osuna, who died tragically in an air crash in June, 1969, had suffered Laver's all-or-nothing attacks in the semi-finals and had said later, 'You have to be a magician to get the ball past Rocket when he is in that kind of form.'

Emerson is great but not a magician and so for two sets he was like a cork tossed in a heavy sea.

Remembering that such a fast start normally leads to a let down, Laver was mentally adjusted to it when it came – in the third set. But he had several wins over Emerson before that final and so retained sufficient dominance to win 6 – 2, 6 – 4, 5 – 7, 6 – 4 and receive congratulations from a host of tennis notabilities headed by the man with whom he now shared the record, Don Budge.

He should have been on top of the world and to some extent was but Laver loves tennis and is a perfectionist. Though now a 'grand slammer' Laver realised that he had not overcome the best and so decided to sign a professional contract for $110,000 immediately after the 1962 Davis Cup Challenge Round.

His professional debut scarcely set the world on fire. Though at peak fitness and match tightness following the Challenge Round, Laver could not contain Lew Hoad when they met in his professional début at Sydney's White City on Saturday, 5th January, 1963, Hoad winning 6 – 8, 6 – 4, 6 – 3, 8 – 6. One day later he met Ken Rosewall who romped home 6 – 3, 6 – 3, 6 – 3. Of the first match Laver said, 'That was the toughest I've ever had and Lew is certainly the best player I have ever met. This professional game is certainly going to be tough but I think I can succeed. I know I have to tighten up several parts of my game to beat these fellows.' His analysis of Rosewall was terse and to the point, 'It is like hitting against a brick wall.'

Seven matches in succession ended in defeat before Laver gained his first win, Rosewall proving the victim. This remained the pattern for the first three months, Laver winning against Hoad or Rosewall only about once in every five meetings. He found the conditions tiring and his confidence faltered. When he competed in the world's major professional tournament at Wembley in the September he went down easily to Buchholz, yet he remained full of faith in his own ability to succeed in the professional game.

He sorely needed more depth on his second services. 'In this company if you do not hit your second serve deep and hard they begin to run round it, start coming in and generally putting the pressure on' he explained : 'If you are not volleying well or confidently then they force you into making errors. You only need two or three errors like that in indoor tennis and they have broken through. Then they can hold serve quite easily to win the set.'

Of passing shots he said 'It is a case of playing a little more, becoming more accurate and getting more sure of yourself.' He found the travelling difficult and wrote in *Lawn Tennis* 'In America when we had two cars which were bought by the association for travelling around there were six of us and two wives. It was tiring when we had to drive ourselves and then play the next night. We played eight or ten matches on consecutive nights, drove three or four hundred miles a day and it started to tell although Ken and I almost had one car to ourselves.'

Towards the end of the year he showed he had assimilated some of the lessons and when the various rankings were published he invariably rated third behind Rosewall and Hoad. By now Hoad's back and right foot were giving him considerable trouble and his form gradually deteriorated. Continuing to benefit from intensive play at top level, Laver progressed steadily but the last steps right at the top are far harder than the first hundred at the start of a competitive career. When 1964 ended he was still behind Rosewall.

By now Open tennis – that is tennis in which amateurs and professionals compete in the same tournaments – had become inevitable and the only doubt was when. The campaign was led strongly by the All England Club, Wimbledon, and they sounded the way by staging a professional tournament on the hallowed centre court towards the end of August, 1967. Back in the environment where the world had first recognised his full potential eight years previously, Laver again blossomed, winning the event with a good deal to spare. Six weeks later the British Lawn Tennis Association threw their bomb into the international scene by announcing that, come what may, they would be staging Open tournaments in 1968.

After loud chest beatings and threats of Britain's world ostracisation by the International Lawn Tennis Federation, the rule permitting Open tennis, albeit on a limited scale, was passed on 30th March, 1968 and Wimbledon was legally open to all categories.

It was expected that the contract professionals would overwhelm all opposition but this was far from the case, many of the household names going down to eager, 'all to gain, nothing to lose' amateurs.

Laver was not among them, his superb techniques and temperament allowing him to quell the fierce serving Negro Arthur Ashe 7 – 5, 6 – 2, 6 – 4 in the semi-finals and the tenacious, gifted Tony Roche 6 – 3, 6 – 4, 6 – 2 in the final.

Of Wimbledon Laver wrote 'There were many moments of anxiety, especially against Denny Ralston, but I was trying all the year to pace myself for a peak at this time and I think I succeeded pretty well.

'The professionals will not be under such great pressure in the opens that follow. Now it will be the amateurs who will have to live up to their record. They have got to prove they can keep on doing it.

'I had no thoughts about the cheque out on court. On court all I think about is winning the match.'

Laver proved an expert prophet, for in the following year, 1969, he was even more dominant, completing the first Open 'grand slam' and becoming the first man to sweep all the majors twice.

In the first nine months of the year his winnings totalled $106,000 and there was no one really capable of replacing him in the biggest events even though he sometimes let down in lesser competitions. Not deliberately, as he explains so often, but through sheer physical inability to maintain peak keenness twelve months out of every twelve.

Tennis elbow, too, which necessitated special treatment every day, also imposed difficulties. Yet in all the major events Laver paced himself so skilfully that he ended each at the very top of his form.

He survived fields stronger in depth and more dangerous in their extremes than any met by previous champions in tennis history. Evolution is painfully slow. There is a tree which 'proves' that the first Wimbledon champion Spencer Gore would have beaten Laver.

Breaking into that tree at the half-way stage provides strong supporting evidence for those who nominate Bill Tilden as the all-time 'Mr Tennis'. Yet the inescapable conclusion to be drawn from Laver's results on the main centre courts of a world condensed by jet travel is that he tops them all.

Logically, evolution should bring forward even greater champions in years to come but of all the men who have so far had tennis demands imposed on them by the competitions and conditions of their day, none has fulfilled those demands better than Rodney Laver. None has fulfilled them more sportingly. None has been better rewarded financially.

Not only financially for, as he says so often and so sincerely, nothing gives him greater pleasure than getting out on a court and playing tennis. But in looking back at the 'greats' who are the heroes of this book, hasn't that been the highest common factor of all? Maybe love of tennis is inborn and cannot be taught. Yet the effect it plays in success suggests it might be wise to make the effort.

Index